Computer Programming for Beginners

Fundamentals of Programming Terms and Concepts

Nathan Clark

Complementary Books

PYTHON

Programming Basics for Absolute Beginners

a. FREE Kindle Version with Paperback

C++

Programming Basics for Absolute Beginners

a. FREE Kindle Version with Paperback

JAVA

Programming Basics for Absolute Beginners

a. FREE Kindle Version with Paperback

C#

Programming Basics for Absolute Beginners

a, FREE Kindle Version with Paperback

JAVASCRIPT

Programming Basics for Absolute Beginners

a, FREE Kindle Version with Paperback

SQL

Programming Basics for Absolute Beginners

a, FREE Kindle Version with Paperback

Table of Contents

Introduction

Welcome to your first steps into the world of programming. This guide has specifically been created for someone who is completely new to programming. We will cover all the concepts, terms, programming paradigms and coding techniques that every beginner should know, and other guides assume you already do. From program structure to error handling, from web programming to data management, and everything in-between.

This guide is the perfect primer to learning any programming language. After creating beginner guides for some of the most popular programming languages, I received several requests to create a guide that precedes those guides and explains the basic concepts of programming. So here it is! I have taken everything a complete novice needs to know, and crammed it into this guide.

This comprehensive guide doesn't focus on merely one specific language, but rather the principles that apply to all programming languages. The emphasis has been placed on detailed descriptions, supported by working code samples from the most popular languages to help illustrate concepts and terms.

This guide will form the foundation for all future programming languages you may encounter. I have put a lot of love and care into this guide, and I hope you enjoy it!

1. What Is a Programming Language?

A programming language is a language that has a set of instructions, that is designed to give a desired output. Programming languages are used to give instructions to the underlying computer they run on. The computer in turn processes the information and then provides the desired output.

With a programming language, we would then develop a set of instructions known as a program. This program would be designed based on a set of requirements. Let's say we wanted to create a system that could handle the purchase orders created by a company. We could then write a program in the programming language of our choice to achieve this.

The programming language itself would be based on a set of constructs, and we would need to create the program based on these constructs. There is a wide range of programming languages available, and it's always wise to choose the right language based on the type of program we want to create. For example, let's say that we wanted to create a system that could work on the internet and be accessible through an internet browser. We would then choose a language that has the necessary capabilities we need, which also function on the internet.

Some of the features that define a good programming language are:

- Simplicity – This refers to the ease of use of the programming language. If the language is easy to use, it becomes more popular amongst the various communities. If a language is hard to learn, it becomes more difficult for people to adopt that language and its usage will drop.

- Functionality – The programming language should be able to cater to the wide variety of functionality required by programs. For example, if we wanted to create a web-based application, then that programming language should have all the features that allow it to work on the internet. Or if we wanted to create a simple component that could be plugged into another system, then the programming language should be able to have the functionality to create pluggable components.

- Structure – A good programming language should have the necessary constructs to create a well-defined and structured program. A cluttered program is difficult to maintain. Hence a properly defined and structured program is always desirable.

- Efficiency – This refers to how well the program runs on the computer. This is an important concept. There is a no point in creating a program and then having the program behave inefficiently when running. Luckily, most programming languages are created with performance in mind. Since many users normally run more than one program at a time, it is important for the language to function as efficiently as possible.

- Continuous updates – Since our environment changes continuously, it has become important that updates are applied continuously to programming languages as well. If new concepts are introduced, then these concepts should also be present in the programming language. Nowadays there are numerous open communities and forums that lend a hand in updating core features of a language.

- Deployment – How easy a program can be deployed is also vital, along with the ability to deploy it on multiple platforms. For example, a program that runs on Windows might not be able to run on Mac OS. In such a case, it becomes important to ensure that the underlying programming language can cater to working on multiple platforms.

- Multiple devices – The programming language should also have the ability to create programs that can run on multiple devices. Nowadays, people prefer to work on mobile devices rather than computers. Hence, programming languages must be able to create programs that work on both traditional computer systems and mobile devices.

- Purpose – Each programming language must have an intended purpose. It's not enough to have a programming language for the sake of having it. Many programming languages are built for a specific purpose. For example in manufacturing industries, we would find programming languages that are built specially to create programs for that industry.

- Compactness – Ideally, a program should be as concise as possible. Having a large program to carry out a minor function does not only lead to performance issues, but also maintainability issues. In such a case, the programming language should be able to provide constructs and structures that can be used to create programs that are concise and to the point.

- Human translation – When we create a program, we want it to emulate exactly what we want it to do. Hence the program should be able to understand what we are trying to make it do. This means that the programming language should have the facility to represent real-world objects. For example, if we wanted to represent a person in a program via a name, then the language should have the necessary statements to define this representation.

2. Why Do We Need a Programming Language?

Over the years, computers have become irreplaceable in our daily lives. They were initially only used in large organization for computing purposes, but are now even being used by children for gaming and social media. The original intended use of the computer was for its power to execute computational instructions. These instructions, which would normally have taken a human days or weeks to execute, could be done by a computer within a fraction of a second.

In order to ensure that the computer could understand what we wanted it to do, we had to give it a predefined set of instructions. These instructions could then be executed by the computer. But in order to create that set of instructions, we needed to have a language of some kind. And that was the advent of programming languages. The programming language could then be used to create a set of instructions that could be understood by the underlying computer system.

Some of the other reasons why a programming language is so important are:

- When we create instructions for the computer to follow, we need to do it in a language that we are familiar with. Computers only recognize instructions in binary language, and it would take ages for a human to create a program in binary code. The programming language would then have the duty of taking this program and converting it to a language that could be understood by the underlying computer system.

- We can also use a programming language to express objects that we use in our daily lives. For example, if we wanted to store the name and age of a person, we could do that using a programming language. That language would have the necessary syntax and constructs to ensure that real-world data can be represented using a simple program.

- Programs can also be used to express relationships between objects. Let's say we wanted to know what items were purchased by a specific individual in a company. We could store and track this with a simple program, and then extrapolate the information in a meaningful way. Most programming languages nowadays allow us to represent objects and also express the relationship between them.

- There are so many different systems out there in today's world, that we need to ensure that data is made available across various systems. Data should be able to travel across systems and be made available whenever required. This can be implemented easily with a program, and we need to have a programming language that can create these programs.

- Programs are also not limited to running only on computers, if we look at the number of smartphones and tablets being used today. So how can we represent what we want to show on a mobile device? We can do this with the help of a program that is compatible with mobile devices. But since the architecture of a mobile device is completely different to that of a traditional computer, we need to have a programming language that can understand how the mobile device works. The language could then make the program run on the particular mobile device.

- Many industries need programs in order to do business on a daily basis. Right from manufacturing facilities with automated production lines, to law firms that use office and accounting software. We can see programs running in almost every part of the world, but for each of these dimensions the programming language needs to be different. It needs to understand how that particular dimension of the industry works. And hence we need programming languages in different spaces to create different types of programs.

Nowadays it is impossible to imagine a life without programs or programming languages. As technology advances, so does the need for a programming language to represent the advances in technology. Some languages are more widely adopted than others, and this all depends on how well the programming language can fit its intended purpose.

3. The History of Programming Languages

The first type of programming languages were known as first generation programming languages. These were languages that were actually written in binary form, which could be understood by computers. The problem with this type of programming language is that you had to have an in-depth understanding of computers and be able to manage the memory allocation.

The subsequent level of programming, or second generation, was known as "Assembly Language Programming". These programs were more readable and did not have to be coded in binary. But again for this set of programming languages, you needed understand the underlying architecture of the machine it would run on.

The very first popular high-level programming language was a language known as FORTRAN. It was invented by IBM, and was made to design programs that could run on the world's fastest supercomputers of the time. It was used to develop programs in compute-intensive environments, such as numerical weather prediction, finite element analysis, computational fluid dynamics, computational physics and crystallography.

Then from the 1960's to the 1970's a great deal of low-level programming languages were developed. Some of these were:

- APL (A Programming Language), which introduced array programming and influenced functional programming.

- ALGOL which was a structured procedural language.

- Lisp, which was the first dynamically typed functional language.

- Simula, which was the first language designed to support object-oriented programming.

- C, which was developed between 1969 and 1973 as a system language for the Unix operating system and still remains a popular language to date.

Then came the age of object-oriented programming languages during the 1980's. During this time C++ was introduced as an object-oriented language, and was also used for systems programming. Following this, came the growth of the Internet and the adoption of websites. Naturally there had to be programming languages that could support the applications built on the Internet. Perl was one of the first languages used for building dynamic websites. It was initially intended for the Unix platform, but then branched out to support dynamic web applications.

The subsequent fourth generation of programming languages had additional support for database management, report generation, mathematical optimization, GUI development, and web development. Some of the general purpose fourth generation languages were Visual FoxPro, PowerBuilder and Uniface.

The fifth generation languages were based on problem solving. Here, constraints were given to the program, rather than using an algorithm written by a program. The reign of each language was dependent on how effective it was at fulfilling its purpose. Some older programming languages are still being used to this day, such as C and C++. At the same time, to keep up with the pace of technology, new programming languages had to be devised. For example with mobile devices, a programming language had to be developed to ensure that compatible programs could be created.

As time progressed, each programming language also had to be updated in order to keep up with technological trends. Java, for instance, has gone through multiple updates and is currently in version 8 at the time of writing this book. Along with programming languages, application and web servers also had to be put in place to run these programs from a central point. So in addition to ensuring the programming languages were regularly updated, the application and web servers that hosted these programs also had to be constantly updated.

At present, we have the advent of Serverless programming. This is where we don't need to provision any infrastructure to run the program. All code is designed to run on a serverless cloud platform.

4. Popular Programming Languages

Now that we have a fair understanding of programming languages, let's look at some of the more popular languages used by developers.

4.1 The C Programming Language

This was one of the earliest languages developed, and many systems were built around the C language. Some of the features of the C programming language are:

- It has a rich set of built-in features and custom functions, which allow developers to create elaborate and complex programs.

- It has numerous functions that can be used to interact with the underlying operating system. For this reason it is used substantially in systems programming.

- Programs written in C are efficient and fast. This is mainly due to its variety of data types and powerful operators.

- It allows for the creation of various modules that can be used to logically separate bits of code.

Even though the C language had many features at the time, the advent of technology brought some pitfalls to light that necessitated a new set of programming languages. One shortcoming of the C language was that the programmer had to properly manage the memory allocation of the program. If this was not managed properly, it would lead to undesirable consequences such as the program crashing unexpectedly.

A significant limitation came with the need for web-enabled programs. The C language did not have the required libraries to work with web programming and hence was mostly used for system and network programming.

4.2 The C# Programming Language

This language was invented by Microsoft to have all the features of C, along with many new concepts. Some of the key features of the C# language are:

- The ability of the environment itself to manage aspects such as memory. Now the memory allocation does not have to be managed by the programmer. Instead, the underlying environment, known as the runtime, would be responsible for allocating and deallocating the memory whenever required.

- It is an object-oriented language, which refers to its ability to create objects that represent real-life entities. The C# language does this with the help of classes and objects. So if we wanted to represent a person in a program, it could be done via the definition of as a class. This class would have properties that could then define the real-life properties of a person, such as their name and surname. Hence each individual could then be represented by creating an object of that class.

- It has the ability to create programs for both desktop and web users. With modern technology, it is no longer realistic to only develop programs that run on the desktop. C# has gained significant popularity because it was designed to run both types of programs.

- It is constantly being maintained by Microsoft and hence there are always updates to this programming language. This means that it will be able to keep up with new technologies, and any shortcomings will likely be addressed as they crop up.

To learn more about programming in C#, be sure to check out our complete series that will take you from beginner to expert in no time.

4.3 The Java Programming Language

This language was initially created by Sun Microsystems, but is now owned by the Oracle Corporation. It has key features that are similar to C#, such as the ability to have classes and objects, as well as memory management. But what makes this language even more popular, is the fact that it is an open source programming language. This allows developers to see how Java works under the hood and contribute to its growth.

Java also allows for its programs to be compatible with almost any platform, by only requiring the equivalent runtime to be installed that pertains to that operating system. While C# was meant to work primarily on the Windows operating system, the Java programs were meant to run on virtually any platform via the Java Runtime Environment.

The Java language also has different editions that focus on specific applications, such as enterprises and mobile platforms. Due to its open source framework, Java has a large support community. Hence if you encounter any problems or issues, you have the support from a large online community.

To learn about the programming versatility of Java, look out for our complete series on Java programming.

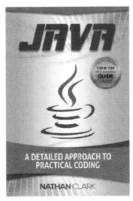

4.4 The JavaScript Programming Language

This is a client scripting language that runs mostly on the user-end in a browser. It is one of the three core technologies the web is based on, along with HTML and CSS. It is used for applications from web pages to video games. JavaScript has truly become one of the most popular languages to date. Some of the key features of the language are:

- It is a lightweight programming language.

- It gives the user more control over what can run in the browser, as well as providing dynamic content in browsers.

- It negates the need for content to be sent to a server to be processed. Normally for client-server applications that use C# or Java, the commands need to be sent to a server for processing. However with JavaScript, most of this can be done locally on the client machine itself, which saves a lot of time.

- It is also an object-oriented language, but differs slightly in the way objects are treated.

- It negates the need to compile a program before submitting the changes, which allows for faster deployment.

To get started in learning how to program in JavaScript, check out our complete series that covers all you need to know to create your own applications.

4.5 The Python Programming Language

This is another extremely popular programming language that is used in a variety of different applications. It is a high-level language that is easy to learn and easy to use. Python has also been around since 1991, and has built up a considerable fanbase. This makes it easy for newcomers to get support when they are stuck or their applications malfunction. Some of the important features of this language are:

- It has a simple language. The code statements used resembles the English language, hence the programs are easier to read and understand.

- It is a free and open source language.

- The programs can be ported to a wide range of operating systems, without the need for major changes.

- It supports procedure-oriented programming and object-oriented programming.

- It has a wide variety of libraries available that can extend the available functionality.

To learn more about programming in one of the most popular languages in the community, be sure to look out for our complete series on Python.

PYTHON

Programming Basics for Absolute Beginners

a FREE Kindle Version with Paperback

4.6 The Angular JS Framework

This is a framework that is built around the JavaScript programming language, and is created and maintained by Google. Many popular websites use this framework to build dynamic websites. Some of the key features of Angular JS are:

- It can be used to develop rich web-based applications.

- It provides an easy way to ensure that data is integrated with business logic code.

- It uses HTML (Hyper Text Markup Language) to build user interfaces.

- It enables developers to write applications with less code.

- It is very easy to test code, due to the Angular framework that was built with unit testing in mind.

4.7 The PHP Programming Language

This is a server-side scripting language that was designed for web development, but is also used for general programming. It is most notably used in combination with web content management systems, web template systems, and a diverse array of web frameworks. Some of the key features of this language are:

- It is very simple and easy to use when compared to other scripting languages.

- It negates the need to compile a program beforehand. This means you don't need to prepare the program for running, you can make changes to the program whenever required and then run the changed program.

- Its programs can be ported to a wide range of operating systems, without the need for major changes.

- It is a free and open source language.

4.8 The Ruby Programming Language

Ruby is defined as a dynamic, reflective, object-oriented, general-purpose language. It is used in combination with a set of libraries known as Rails, which allows for much greater functionality. Some of the key features of this programming language are:

- It is completely free of charge, and can be used, copied and modified quite easily.

- It is an object-oriented programming language.

- It can be used as a server-side scripting language.

- It can be embedded into HTML.

- It has a clean and easy to understand syntax, that makes it easy for new developers to learn.

- It is quite easy to write and maintain complex programs.

5. Understanding the Structure of a Program

Each programming language normally has their own structure and constructs. It is then up to the developer to ensure that they learn the appropriate programming language constructs to develop a program. Generally, all programming languages follow some common practices that help define and structure a program. Let's have a look at some of these principles.

5.1 Blocks of Code

Normally each programming language uses the curly braces, { }, to signify a block of code. This helps to ensure that code is structured and organized in a program.

5.2 Separating Code into Modules

Each programming language has a fundamental way of separating code into modules. This is where logical pieces of code are split and contained inside designated modules. Some of the advantages of splitting code into modules are:

- One advantage of splitting code into modules, is that it makes the code easier to maintain. So if a change has to be made in the functionality of a program, it can be made to only the module that contains the functionality, instead of the entire program.

- It can also be used to ensure loose coupling in a program. This is a way of ensuring the various parts of a program aren't dependent on each other.

- It aids in separating the entire program into different functional modules.

Below is a sample piece of code on how a module looks in the C# language.

```
static void Add()
{
    int i=3;
    int j=4;

    Console.WriteLine("The sum of the integers is "+ (i + j));
}
```

In this sample, the module has the functionality of adding 2 numbers together, and that is the only purpose of the module. The module also has a name and can be invoked at any point in the program via this name.

5.3 Using Data Placeholders

These are normally known as variables in a programming language. They are used to hold values that can then be used during the course of a program. For example, if we have a program that adds 2 numbers, then we would define two data placeholders for these numbers. Let's refer to our code snippet from before:

```
static void Add()
{
    int i=3;
    int j=4;

    Console.WriteLine("The sum of the integers is "+ (i + j));
}
```

Here we have two data placeholders, namely 'i' and 'j'. We then assign values to these placeholders. These values can sometimes change during the course of the program, which is why we use placeholders.

Most programming languages also have a concept known as 'Data Types', which defines the type of data that can be stored by these placeholders. In the above sample the data type is 'int' or Integer, which is a special form of a number. One of the advantages of having data types associated with these placeholders, is that it keeps a strict rule of what type of data the variable can hold.

5.4 Using Classes

Most programming languages also support 'Classes'. This stems from a programming language concept known as 'Object Oriented Programming'. As an example, let's say we have a program that needs to store the name and ID of 20 students. Without the use of classes, we would define 40 data placeholders. Not only is this inefficient, but it is difficult to maintain. Instead, we would define a class with properties.

These properties are nothing more than data placeholders. An example of how this will look in C# is shown below:

```
class Student
{
int studentID;
string studentName;
}
```

In this code, the name of the class is 'Student'. The class also has two data placeholders, namely 'StudentID' and 'studentName', each of which has a data type. Now if we wanted to have the information for the 20 students, we would create something known as objects. These objects would then contain the information of the students.

5.5 Using Repetitive Constructs

Repetitive constructs are used whenever there is a need to repeat certain lines of code, a certain number of times. Most programming languages have constructs in place that can do this. Below is an example of a repetitive statement in Java.

```
int i=0;
do
{
    System.out.println("The value of i is "+ i);
    i++;
}
while(i<4);
```

In the above code, there is a need to execute the following line multiple times:

```
System.out.println("The value of i is "+ i);
```

This type of repetition is achieved with a loop construct, known as a 'do-while' loop. There are many different loops in each programming language. In a loop construct we also usually have a condition that needs to be met. Only once the condition evaluates to true, will the loop be iterated a specified number of times. In our prior example, the condition is that the value of 'i' should be less than 4.

5.6 Using Decision Statements

Decision statements are used whenever there is a need to perform a decision task in a program. Most programming languages have the constructs in place that can do this. Below is an example of a decision statement in Java.

```
if (i < 5) {
System.out.println("The value of i is less than 5");
}
```

In this code, the 'if' decision statement verifies a condition. Only if the condition evaluates to true, will the statement execute.

5.7 Evaluating Errors

Another common programming practice which lends to the structure of a program is the checking of errors. Errors are also sometimes known as 'Exceptions'. Our primary goal is to attempt to catch errors as early as possible in the program execution. This ensures that the program can continue running without being interrupted. Below is an example of how errors can be caught in Java.

```
try {
    int[] arr=new int[3];
    arr[4]=1;
}
catch (Exception exp) {
    System.out.println("An exception has occurred");
}
```

The above piece of code consists of three main statements:

- try - This block identifies a block of code in which the exception can occur. We place our primary code in the try block.

- catch - This block is used to handle the exception if it occurs.

- finally - This block is used to execute a given set of statements, whether an exception occurs or not.

6. What Are the Different Types of Programs?

There are different types of programs that can be created for different purposes. Normally each programming language would have the ability to create all, or most, of these types of programs. Let's have a look at the different categories of programs that can be created.

6.1 Web Applications

This is probably the most common type of program. The primary goal is to have a program that can be accessed via a web browser. Due to the widespread availability of high-speed internet, web applications have grown considerably in popularity and necessity. Almost all programming languages support the development of web-based programs. Some distinct advantages of web applications are:

- There is no need to install any software on the client's machine.

- There is no need to download any software.

- Most of the processing is done on the server side.

One consideration to keep in mind is that in order for the web program to work, it needs to be hosted on a web application server. For example, when using C# we would need to host software known as Internet Information Services on a server to make the program accessible over the internet. Some other aspects that should be looked at when developing a web program are:

- Storage of data – Data storage is an important aspect of any web application. Let's assume we have a website that sells items online. We would need a data store in order to store the information pertaining to the items being sold on the website. This data store would be a separate entity, but still maintain a connection with the web application.

- Storage of user information –To create a better user experience, some web applications might store user preferences. So when users return to the web program, they would get the same experience they had when they visited the program earlier. This can be done by storing something known as cookies on the client machine, or storing cookies as a separate entity on the server.

- Design for performance – Since most web programs are created to be used by multiple users, they should be designed for maximum performance and efficiency. If the environment that hosts the program becomes unstable due to bad programming practices, it could affect all the users who are accessing the application.

- Security – Web applications are designed primarily to run over the internet which makes security a critical aspect, especially when we are working with commercial based web programs. Applications should hence be designed to protect the information being transferred.

- Device compatibility – These days, applications are accessed on a variety of different devices other than just traditional computers. Because of this, programs should be developed with all these devices in mind and how the application will function on these devices.

- Being mindful of changes – Since web programs are used by multiple users, care should be taken when changes are made to the program. So when changes are implemented to address one group of users, we should also consider how these changes will affect all possible users.

6.2 Client-Server Applications

These types of programs are developed to run primarily on a local machine. When compared to web applications, they tend to require more resources than a typical web program. So if a program needs to have extremely high end functionality and processing capabilities, then having the program run in a web browser may not be the ideal approach. In such a case, having a client-server program is preferred.

An example of a client-server application is an Enterprise Resource Planning system. The client software is installed on each user's system, and then interacts with a server software for data related artifacts. Normally these types of applications are transactional-based systems, wherein each client would make calls and changes to data on a server-based system. Some of the disadvantages of these types of programs are:

- Since the client program has a lot of functionality built in, it can become somewhat bulky and difficult to maintain.

- The client program also needs to be installed for every user, and constantly updated for every installation.

6.3 Scripting Programs

Scripting programs are used for automating tasks, and are built to perform a specific task. As an example, if we have a requirement to create a daily backup of a data source, we could simply create a script to perform this task. Some of the advantages of developing such programs are:

- The script is generally short, hence it is easier to develop and maintain than a full blown application.

- Since the requirements are very specific, it is easy to finalize a project and move on to the next one.

Since scripting programs are simple to create, it could lead to developers creating a great deal of scripts to automate tasks. This could in turn become a nightmare to maintain.

7. How Is a Program Built?

In most programming languages, we need to perform a process of building a program before it can be executed. This process normally involves something known as compilation and then the subsequent building of the program. So what exactly is the compilation process? This process basically checks the program for any form of syntactical errors.

No program is perfect, and there can always be a case where a program is built with constructs that don't conform to the underlying programming language. Normally every programming language has a separate program or software known as the compiler. When a program needs to be built, it is submitted to the compiler which then checks the program for any sorts of errors.

In Java, the compiler is a program known as 'javac.exe' (pronounced "java-see"). So whenever a program needs to be compiled, it is submitted to the javac compiler program. As an example, let's say we have a program called 'HelloWorld.java' that is written in the Java programming language. In order to build the program, we would need to execute the following command:

```
javac HelloWorld.java
```

This command first checks the program for any sort of errors. Now let's say we have the following program that needs to be compiled:

```
public class HelloWorld {
    public static void main(String[] args) {
        // Prints "Hello, World" to the terminal window.
        System.out.printl("Hello, World");
    }
}
```

To understand the compilation process, we have specified the wrong name for the 'println' function in the above code and will now submit this program to the compiler. If this is done, we will get the following output:

HelloWorld.java:5: error: cannot find symbol
System.out.printl("Hello, World");
               ^
symbol: method printl(String)
location: variable out of type PrintStream
1 error

From the above, we can see that the compiler is showing an error on a particular line and hence cannot continue with the execution of the program. The compiler performs a critical function by ensuring that programs are free from syntactical errors before being executed.

7.1 Compiler in the IDE

Normally the compiler program is incorporated in the Integrated Development Environment (or IDE), which is used for developing programs. This helps the developer in creating and compiling programs on the fly. Below is a snapshot of the Visual Studio IDE, which is used for developing programs in C#. Here the compiler is built into the IDE itself. So when we try to build a program that contains an error, it will come up in the error list. This feature can be found in most IDE's.

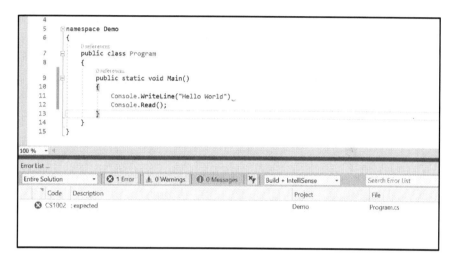

7.2 Compiling Dependencies

Normally when we create a program and it grows in size, it is preferable to split the program into smaller sections. We then compile each portion separately, to make sure it works as intended. When the entire program is eventually merged, we need to ensure that all of the smaller programs are included in the compiler process, or else the program will fail to compile.

We are essentially ensuring that the dependencies of the program are in place. This is a very common practice in the world of programming. As an example, a key program is excluded from the main program in the snapshot below, which will result in a compilation error.

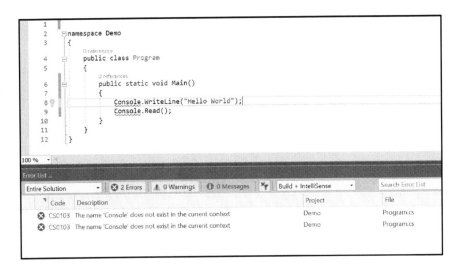

The concept of including dependent programs has become so complex in many cases, that special software has been developed to ensure all dependent packages and programs are present in the program. One such program is called NuGet. This is a package manager for .Net programs, and is responsible for downloading and maintaining packages and dependent programs for the .Net environment.

7.3 Program Translation

Another function of the compiler is to ensure that the program is translated into a language that can be understood by the system that will be running the program. This differs from language to language. When a Java program is compiled, it is converted to a class file that has the same name as the Java program file. For example, if we have a program named 'HelloWorld.java' and ran the command below to compile the program:

```
javac HelloWorld.java
```

Another file would be created called 'HelloWorld.class'. This is the file that will be submitted to the subsequent program for running on the target system. The '.class' file contains the necessary instructions based on the main program, which allows it to be executed on the underlying operating system. So if a program needs to run on Windows, the '.class' file will then contain the instructions that can be understood by the Windows operating system.

7.4 Immediate Compilation

Nowadays we have access to underlying programming languages and frameworks where the compilation process can happen automatically. One such framework is the Angular JS language. Here, the underlying engine that runs the Angular JS program has the ability to detect changes on the fly and then compile and run the new version of the program. Some of the core advantages of this are:

- Faster deployment. Since we don't need to compile the program we can make changes directly and it will be deployed.

- We can deploy many changes, more frequently.

A key disadvantage of this technique is that we could deploy the wrong changes. Since there is always a chance that we might make mistakes, having the changes happen automatically could be disastrous. What's even worse is that the incorrect change could be reflected to all users. Hence when using these programming languages, extra precaution should be taken when making changes to the underlying program.

8. How Is a Program Executed?

In the last section, we saw the various aspects that go into a program being compiled and built. Next, we'll look at how a program is executed. The way in which a program gets executed depends on the type of program and the type of programming language. Each language has more or less the same principles, but there are still some subtle differences on how the program gets executed.

It is important to understand the various parameters that are required to ensure a program executes. Traditionally, programmers only had knowledge on how to develop the program. But when it came to executing and deploying the program on a large scale, they encountered some difficulty. Lately it has become important for all developers to not only understand how to develop a program, but also how to execute and deploy a program.

Some of the important considerations for program execution are:

- Will the program run as a standalone program?

- Will the program run as a centralized program that will be accessed by many users? In so, does a web program seem more feasible?

- Will the program be executed on different devices, such as mobiles?

All of these parameters are crucial in having the program execute successfully. Let's look at the execution of a program for the various types of programs available.

8.1 Client Based Programs

These are programs that are designed to run on the user's system. All the logic and processing for the program happen on the client's side. A separate program is also required most of the time, in order to run the program. For example, if we have a program that is built in Java, we will use a software called 'Java Runtime Environment' to run the program on the user's system.

The Java Runtime Environment (or JRE) is available for different operating systems. So if the program is intended to run on a Windows machine, we would need to install the JRE for the Windows operating system. The Java Runtime Environment would run in the background and then execute the necessary Java program. Similarly, when running a program created in C#, we would need to install the .Net runtime environment.

8.2 Web Based Programs

When working with web-based programs, we need to have a separate machine running a software for hosting the web program. The general process for setting up a web-based program is:

- First we set up a separate machine to host the web-based software.

- Next we install the web-based software on this machine. When using C#, we would install a software known as Internet Information Services.

- We compile and build the web-based program.

- We deploy the web-based program on this machine.

- Finally, we get a URL that can be used by all users to access the web-based program.

When running a program on a centralized server, there are several important aspects to keep in mind:

- Ensure the right settings are used for the hosting program, as this can influence numerous users that connect to the server.

- Pay special attention to the required specifications of the hosting machine. This generally depends on the number of users that will be accessing the hosted web program. A high number of users would necessitate a high-end machine to handle the traffic.

- Since the web program will be used by multiple users, it is important to design the program with performance and efficiency in mind. If the environment that hosts the program becomes unstable due to bad programming practice, it would negatively affect all the users that are accessing the web program.

- Ensure that communication with the hosting server is secure. In this day and age where data can be tampered with quite easily, it is important to take additional precaution when sending data over the web.

8.3 Scripting Programs

These are the easiest programs to deploy and execute. This is due to the programs not needing any special software or procedures to run on the underlying system. Since most of these programs are generally built directly on the system they are intended to run on, they can be deployed effortlessly.

8.4 Mobile Based Programs

For programs to be executed on a mobile device, the program needs to be developed in a programming language that is geared towards mobile development. There is software available, such as Android Studio, which helps in the development of mobile-based programs. They have numerous features, such as running the program on a virtual mobile device, to visualize how it would look and feel when executed on a real device.

9. What Are Program Statements?

When a program is created using a programming language, it is constructed with the use of statements. Each statement is an instruction on what the program is meant to do. These statements are then taken by the compiler and converted to a language that can be understood by the operating system. There are different types of statements in a programming language. Let's look at some examples.

```
Console.Write("Hello World");
```

The above statement is an example taken from C#. Its purpose is to display the string 'Hello World' when the program is run. Let's look at the various parts of this statement:

- The statement starts by setting the location where the string needs to be displayed, and that is the 'Console' of the program.

- The next part of the statement uses a method called 'Write', which is used to take the string and display it to the console.

- Now since this statement makes use of a method, it needs to enclose the string within the '(' and ')' brackets.

- Next is the string that needs to be displayed to the console.

- And finally is a termination of the statement using the semi-colon ';'.

When the compiler receives this statement, it will break it into various parts (also known as tokens). Each token is then placed in a respective area in the memory when the program is being executed. Let's look at another example of a statement.

```
class Program
```

This statement above is very simple. Its purpose is to tell the compiler that the next lines of code, which will come after this statement, will be part of a class called Person. Normally methods and classes are embedded within the opening and closing curly braces and shown below. The code that is enclosed within the opening and closing curly braces then becomes part of the class program.

```
class Program
  {
  //code
  }
```

Now let's look at an assignment statement. Most programming languages have the same format for assignment statements. These statements are normally used to assign values to literals.

```
i=5;
```

In the above statement we have a variable called 'i'. The statement then assigns a value of 5 to the variable 'i'. Normally assignment statements are used to assign values to variables during the course of the program.

```
if (i==10)
{
//code
}
```

Above is an example of a conditional statement; or more specifically an 'if' conditional statement. In this statement we first have the 'if' keyword, which indicates the type of conditional statement, followed by the condition itself. In our example, the first line of code checks if the value of 'i' is equal to 10.

Then based on the outcome of the condition, we execute a set of statements. These statements are enclosed in the opening and closing curly braces that follow the condition. In our example, if the value of 'i' is equal to 10 the program will execute '//code'.

```
while (count < 10)
{
//code
}
```

Next let's look at loop iteration statements. These types of statements are used to iterate through a set of statements a certain number of times. In the statement above we first have the 'while' keyword that indicates iteration, followed by the condition and then the code block to execute. In our example, as long as the variable 'count' is less than 10, the '//code' statement will be executed. And it will continue to be executed, until the count is 10 or higher.

```
int i;
```

The above statement is a declaration statement. They are used to declare identifiers in a program. In this instance, it is used to declare an identifier called 'i' as an 'integer'. There are many different data types available for identifiers. We will look at this in greater detail in the Data Types chapter.

```
Comments
```

Next we have the comments statement shown above. This is used to declare statements that will not be executed. They are purely used for leaving notes and to help make a program more maintainable in future. This is a great way to remind yourself what a specific section of code's purpose is when you refer back to it later. And if someone else works on your program in the future, they can also understand the intent was. Let's look at an example of this.

```
// This is a statement to write hello world to the console
Console.Write("Hello World");
```

Here the double forward slash keyword '//' is used to denote that a comment statement is being used and that the line will not form part of the executing program. This is an example of a single comment statement. We can also denote a multiple comment statement by enclosing the comment with a forward slash asterisk '/*' before, and an asterisk forward slash '*/' after, the comment as shown below.

```
/* This is a statement to write Hello world to the console
In this statement , we are going to use the Console statement */
Console.Write("Hello World");
```

Below is a snippet of a program in C# that makes use of the various statements we discussed. This program is used to display 'Hello World', and is one of the first programs most languages will teach.

```
using System;
namespace Demo
{
  // A simple application using C#
    class Program
  {
    // The main function
    static void Main(string[] args)
    {
      // Displaying Hello world to the console
      Console.Write("Hello World");
      Console.Read();
    }
  }
}
```

10. What Are Data Types?

Data types are used to define what type of data is used within a program. Depending on the type of data that needs to be stored, the computer would then allocate the necessary memory for it. Normally there are two ways in which data can be stored. It can be done either directly or via pointers.

The simplest way of storing data is directly in the memory location in the system. Alternatively data can be stored in the memory by using a pointer that directs to the memory location. We will look at an illustration of this later on in the chapter. First, let's go over the different data types to understand how each one works.

10.1 Integer Data Type

This data type is used to denote the storage of numbers. Most programming languages allow for storing numbers. The integer data type is normally allocated to an identifier, which then assumes the data type. Below is an example of how this is done in C#.

```
int i;
```

So in this statement, 'i' is known as the identifier and the data type is specified as 'int'. This is the way we would define the integer data type for the identifier. Once this has been done, we can assign a number to the identifier via an assignment statement as shown below.

```
i=5;
```

Here the value of 5 is being assigned to the identifier. Since the identifier 'i' was defined as an integer data type, it cannot be assigned a string such as 'Hello'. There is a separate string data type for this. This is the entire concept of data types, which ensures that the identifier can only assume that data type. If an invalid data type is assigned, it will result in an error.

Some programming languages have two ways in which integers can be defined. One is using the 'int' data type as shown above, and the other is the 'long' data type that is used to denote a larger number. Each data type has a certain number of bytes that are allocated to it for storing the number.

10.2 Double or Float Data Type

This data type is used to denote that the identifier can store a number with a decimal point. Below is an example that shows how an identifier is defined as a float data type in C#. Then we assign a number with a decimal value to the identifier.

```
float f;
f=1.11;
```

Some programming languages have two data types for decimal values, one is 'float' and the other is 'double'. The double data type has a higher precision and can store numbers with a larger number of decimal places.

10.3 Character Data Type

This data type is used to store a single character. Below is an example of how an identifier is defined as a character data type in Java, and then assigned a character.

```
char c;
c='A';
```

10.4 String Data Type

This data type is used to store a string of characters. This is one of the most common data types used in programming. Below is an example of how to define an identifier as a string data type in Java. Then we also assign a string to the identifier.

```
String str;
str="Hello World";
```

10.5 Boolean Data Type

This data type is used to store a Boolean value of 'true' or 'false'. Below is an example of how we can define an identifier as a Boolean data type in Java, along with assigning a Boolean value to the identifier.

```
boolean b;
b=false;
```

Apart from the simple data types we've seen above, there are also complex data types that are used when simple data types just aren't capable of representing the data we require. Let's look at some of these complex data types.

10.6 Structure Data Type

This is a composite data type that is used to hold a set of identifiers. For instance, if we wanted to store information for a set of students via a structure data type, it would look like the sample below when using C#.

```
struct Students
{
    public int ID;
    public String Name;
}
```

Here the keyword 'struct' is used to denote that we are using the structure data type, and the name given to the structure is 'Students'. Then the student data structure has two properties (or identifiers) that have data types assigned to them. 'ID' is defined as integer and 'Name' is defined as string. This structure can then be used to define the information pertaining to the students.

10.7 Class Data Type

This data type is also used to hold a set of properties, but it is more commonly used than structures because it pertains to object-oriented programming. An example of how a class looks in C# is shown below, again using the example of student information.

```
Class Students
{
   public int ID;
   public String Name;
}
```

As with the structure data type, the class has two properties of 'ID' and 'Name', each with their own data type. Some of the main differences between the 'struct' and 'class' data types are:

- We can declare members as 'private' in a class. This prevents the data values stored in the data members from being tampered with.

- Concepts such as Inheritance are also possible in classes, which we will cover later.

10.8 Storing Data Types

Now is a good time to go over the methods of storing data types. With simple data types, such as integers and float data types, the values are normally stored directly in the memory via a stack stored on the system. However, some programming languages store these data types as pointers. In these situations, if we declare a string as we did previously, it would be represented in the memory as follows:

```
str ----> Hello World
```

Here the "Hello World" value is stored in a memory location and the 'str' literal is used to point to the string value.

So if we had to change the value of "Hello World" to a new value, a new memory location would be allocated to the new data value, instead of changing the value in the memory. The 'str' variable would then point to the new data value. The representation of this in memory would be as follows:

```
str ----> New Hello World
          Hello World
```

The original value would still be in memory and the 'str' literal variable would then point to the new memory location. Hence in programming, it is always important to understand how data types are allocated.

11. What Are Variables?

Variables in any programming language are used to hold data that can be used at any time during the course of the program. Normally these variables are listed as identifiers of a particular data type. These variables then hold various values that can be used across all parts of a program. Let's look at an example of a variable in C#.

```
int i;
```

In the above statement, 'i' is the identifier that is of the integer data type. Values can then be assigned to the variable with an assignment statement as shown below

```
i=5;
```

Here the value of 'i' is assigned a value of 5. This variable can then be used during the course of the program. For example, the value attached to this variable could be displayed in the console by means of the following statement:

```
Console.Write(i);
```

In the above statement, when a reference to 'i' is made, the value of 5 will be displayed.

The value assigned to the variable can also be changed at any point in time. Let's look at how easily this can be done.

```
int i;
i=5;
Console.Write(i);
i=10;
Console.Write(i);
```

In this example, we are first declaring the variable 'i'. Then we assign a value of 5 to the variable before displaying the value in the console. We then assign a new value of 10 to the variable, before again displaying the value in the console.

11.1 Constants

There can come a time when we might not want the value of a variable to change during the course of a program. If we want the value to remain constant, we can define the variable as a constant so that the value cannot be changed. In Java, we can do this by defining the variable with the keywords of 'final' and 'static'. This will look like the following:

```
public static final int i = 5;
```

In this example we have the variable 'i', which is assigned the value of 5. But since the variable has been defined as static and final, it means that the value cannot be changed. If we try to change the value during the course of the program, we will get an error message.

11.2 Variable Interactions

The values in variables can also interact with each other. Let's say we have two integer variables and want to add the values of these variables together. This can be done quite easily with simple mathematical addition. An example of how this can be done in C# is shown below.

```
int a=5;
int b=10;
int c=a+b;
```

In this sample code, we assign the value of 5 to the variable 'a' and we assign the value of 10 to the variable 'b'. We then create the variable 'c' and assign it the value of 'a' and 'b'.

11.3 Variable Scope

Some programming languages allow us to define a scope in which variables are not visible to other statements. To understand this better, let's look at the following code in C#:

```
{
    int i=5;
}
Console.WriteLine(i);
```

In this sample code, we first declare and initialize the variable 'i' to a value of 5. But note that we are doing this in a separate code block within curly braces '{ }'. This means that the visibility of this declaration is only within the curly braces, and that the 'Console.Writeline' statement cannot see the variable declaration of 'i'.

So if we run this program it will result in an error. Let's consider the same set of statements and see what would ideally work.

```
{
    int i=5;
    Console.WriteLine(i);
}
```

Now we are ensuring that we also add the 'Console.WriteLine' statement in the enclosed code block, in which the variable 'i' is declared and initialized. The program will now run without error and display the value of 'i' to the console. One big advantage of this arrangement is that we can declare separate variables inside and outside of the code block. Below is an example of this.

```
int j=10;
{
    int i=5;
    Console.WriteLine(i);
}
Console.WriteLine(j);
```

In this example, we declare and access the variable 'i' inside the code block, while in the same program we can access the variable 'j' that we declared outside the code block.

12. What Are Operators?

Operators are used to carry out operations on the data stored in variables. So if we stored numbers in two different variables, we could use operators to perform mathematical tasks on them. There are different types of operators available. Let's look at them in more detail.

12.1 Arithmetic Operators

These types of operators are used to carry out operations on number based variables. Let's look at an example of this in C#.

```
int i = 10;
int j = 3;
int k=i+j;
```

In this sample we are defining three variables: 'i', 'j' and 'k'. When it comes to variable 'k', we are using the addition operator '+' to add the values assigned to 'i' and 'j' together. Most programming languages have access to the operators used to perform normal arithmetic operations. Below is a list of the operators that are normally available.

Arithmetic Operators

Operator	Operation
+	This is used to add two operands
-	This is used to subtract one operand from another
*	This is used to multiply two operands
/	This is used to divide one operand by another
%	This gives the remainder value after a division operator
++	This is used to increment a value by one
--	This is used to decrement a value by one

12.2 Relational Operators

These are operators that are used to compare variables based on their values. Let's look at an example of this in C#.

```
int i = 10;
int j = 3;
Console.WriteLine("Is i equal to j " + (i==j));
```

In this sample we are defining two variables, namely 'i' and 'j', and assigning values to these variables. We are then using a relational operator '==' to compare the values stored in these variables. If the values are equal to one another we will get a response of 'True' or '1', depending on the programming language we are using.

Below is a list of relational operators that are normally available in the various programming languages.

Relational Operators

Operator	Operation
==	This is used to check if two operands are equal
!=	This is used to check if two operands are not equal
>	This is used to check if one operand is greater than another
<	This is used to check if one operand is less than another
>=	This is used to check if one operand is greater than or equal to another
<=	This is used to check if one operand is less than or equal to another

12.3 Logical Operators

These are operators that are used to compare Boolean variables based on their values. Remember that a Boolean variable can only have a 'True' or 'False' value. Let's look at an example of this in C#.

```
Boolean i = true;
Boolean j = true;
Console.WriteLine("i AND j   " + (i&&j));
```

Similar to our previous sample, we are defining two variables, namely 'i' and 'j', and assigning values to these variables. This time around the variables are defined as Boolean instead of integer. We then use a logical operator '&&' to perform the AND operation on the variables. In this instance, because both variables are indeed 'True' we will get a response of 'True'. Below is a list of logical operators which are normally available in the various programming languages.

Logical Operators

Operator	Operation
&&	This is the logical AND operator
||	This is the logical OR operator
!	This is the logical NOT operator

12.4 Assignment Operators

These are operators that are used to make assignment operations easier. We have already seen the simple assignment operator denoted by the equal sign '='. However, we can also combine the assignment and arithmetic operators to execute both at the same time. Let's look at an example of this in C#.

```
int a = 10;
int b;
b = a;
b += a;
```

In this sample we declare a variable 'a' and assign a value to it. We also declare a variable 'b' and assign it the value of 'a' by using the simple assignment operator. Then we assign a new value to 'b' by using the plus equals operator '+='. This assigns a value by adding 'a' and 'b' together. Thus the first value of 'b' would be 10 and the second would be 20. Below is a list of assignment operators which are normally available in the various programming languages.

Assignment Operators

Operator	Operation
=	This is used to assign the value of an operation to an operand
+=	This is used to carry out the addition and assignment operator in one go
-=	This is used to carry out the subtraction and assignment operator in one go
*=	This is used to carry out the multiplication and assignment operator in one go
/=	This is used to carry out the division and assignment operator in one go
%=	This is used to carry out the modulus and assignment operator in one go

12.5 Bitwise Operators

These are operators that are used to perform bit operations on operands. In other words, they perform an action on the bits of a number when converted to binary. As such they are not commonly used in real life. Let's look at an example of this in C#.

```
int i = 14;
int j = 11;
Console.WriteLine("Showcasing the & bit operator  " + (i&j));
```

In this sample we are defining two variables, 'i' and 'j' and assigning values to these variables. We then use the bitwise operator '&' to perform the AND operation on the variables. The process compares the corresponding bits in the binary equivalent of the values we declared. If either of the bits is 0, the result is 0. Otherwise the result is 1.

Number	Binary			
14	1	1	1	0
11	1	0	1	1
Result	**1**	**0**	**1**	**0**

Our binary result of 1010 is then converted to a decimal number, giving us 10. Below is a list of bitwise operators which are normally available in the various programming languages.

Bitwise Operators

Operator	Operation
&	This copies a bit to the result if it exists in both operands
		This copies a bit to the result if it exists in either operands

^	This copies a bit to the result if it exists in one operands but not in both
<<	Here the left operands value is moved left by the number of bits specified by the right operand
>>	Here the left operands value is moved right by the number of bits specified by the right operand

13. Working with Numbers

Working with numbers is an integral part of any programming language. The initial need for computers, and their computational power, was to work with complex numbers. For this reason, most languages have the ability to work with an array of numbers.

In programming languages, a number is represented by a number of bits. It is this number of bits that determines what range of values can be stored in that number. A number is also defined by a specific data type, as we discussed earlier. This data type will determine what type of number can be stored in a variable.

To illustrate the above concepts, let's look at the 'short' data type used in C#. This data type can store 16 bits, which translates to a number range of 216 or 65,536. Since this data type can store negative as well as positive numbers, the range of values it can store is from -32,768 to 32,767. Numbers can also be constituted as whole or decimal values, and most languages have the facility to work with decimals.

13.1 Operations on Numbers

Number operations are probably the most common and most used aspects when working with numbers. Most programming languages make provision for basic number operators. The table below provides examples of the operators available in Java.

Arithmetic Operators

Operator	Operation
+	This is used to add two operands
-	This is used to subtract one operand from another
*	This is used to multiply two operands
/	This is used to divide one operand by another
%	This gives the remainder value after a division operator
++	This is used to increment a value by one
--	This is used to decrement a value by one

As you can see, we've covered these operators in the previous chapter. However, let's look at a quick example again by using Java.

```
int a=2;
int b=3;
int c=a+b;
```

In this sample we are defining three variables as integers. We also assign the values of 2 and 3 to variables 'a' and 'b'. Then we use the addition operator '+' to add these values together and store the result in variable 'c'.

70

13.2 Number Functions

Programming languages also provide additional functions that can be used when working with numbers. These functions provide common functionality that is present in many spreadsheet applications. For example, if we wanted to find the greatest value between two or more numbers, many programming languages have a built-in function for this. In C#, we would use the 'max' function that is part of a 'math' library, as shown below.

```
using System;
namespace Demo
{
    class Program
    {
        // The main function
        static void Main(string[] args)
        {
            // Defining a number
            double a = 10;
            double b = 20;
            // Using the max function
            Console.WriteLine("The value is " + Math.Max(a,b));
            Console.Read();
        }
    }
}
```

In the above program, we are first defining two numbers with values of 10 and 20 respectively. Then we use the 'Math.Max' function to find the maximum value out of these numbers and output the result to the console. In a similar way, there are many more functions available for common operations. These functions reduce the amount of programming needed by developers, because the functions are built into the programming language.

14. The Importance of Strings

A string is another important type of data that can be stored by programs. Almost all data contains strings in one form or another, and hence every programming language has the ability to work with strings. A string is simply a series of characters or text. Below is an example of a string definition in C#.

```
string str = "Hello";
```

In this sample, 'string' denotes the data type, 'str' is the variable name we chose, and 'Hello' is the value given to the variable. In most programming languages, strings are immutable. This means that the value of the string technically cannot be modified. In reality it cannot be modified in the memory, but we can assign a new value to the variable. To illustrate, have a look at the following code:

```
string str = "Hello";
str="Hello World";
```

We are assigning a value of 'Hello' to the variable, and then assigning a new value of 'Hello World' to the same variable. So what is happening behind the scenes?

73

The programming language uses the variable 'str' as a pointer, which points to a memory location in the system. The memory location is then populated with the value of 'Hello'. When we change the value of the variable, a new memory location is populated with the value of 'Hello World'. The 'str' pointer is then made to point to the new memory location. The earlier memory location now has no pointer, and in most programming languages the contents will be deleted.

14.1 Concatenation of Strings

Combining strings is a very common practice in programming. Normally the easiest way to combine strings is to use the addition '+' operator, and most programming languages allow the concatenation of strings using this operator. Below is an example of this in C#.

```
string str ="Hello"+" World";
```

Here we have two strings being combined into one string, resulting in 'Hello World', and then assigned to the 'str' variable. This is the easiest way to quickly combine strings. However programming languages also have built-in functions and methods that can do this. For example, C# has a method called 'StringBuilder' that can be used to build and combine strings.

14.2 Properties and Methods on Strings

Just like we have seen with numbers, there are also properties and methods available in most programming languages to work with strings. Again, these built-in methods help in performing the most common tasks needed with strings. For example to determine the number of characters in a string, most programming languages have the 'length' property that can be used for this purpose. An example of this in C# is shown below.

```
using System;
namespace Demo
{
    class Program
    {
        // The main function
        static void Main(string[] args)
        {
            // Defining a string
            string str = "Hello";
            Console.WriteLine("The length is " + str.length);
            Console.Read();
        }
    }
}
```

In this sample we have a string with a variable named 'str' and it is assigned the value of 'Hello'. Then we use the 'length' property to determine the number of characters in this string, and write that number to the console. As mentioned, there are numerous methods available to use with strings. Let's look at some of them next.

14.2.1 Searching in Strings

Let's say we wanted to find a particular word in a string. This can be done quite easily with the use of methods. For example, C# has the 'contains' method built in that is made for this exact purpose. If the string contains the desired letter or word, the program will return a 'true' value. Let's look at an example of this.

```
namespace Demo
{
  class Program
  {
    // The main function
    static void Main(string[] args)
    {
      // Defining a string
      string str = "Hello";
      // Using the Contains function
      Console.WriteLine("String contains e " + str.Contains("e"));
      Console.Read();
    }
  }
}
```

14.2.2 Finding the Position of a Character

We can also find the position value of a character in a particular string by using methods. For instance, Java has the 'indexOf' method built in that can be used for this exact purpose. If a string contains the desired character, the program will return the index number of that character.

```
public class Demo {
  public static void main(String args[]) {
    // Defining the string
    String str="Hello World";
    System.out.println("The index is " + str.indexOf('e'));
  }
}
```

Normally strings start with an index value of 0. So in our example, if the program returns a value of 1, the character is positioned second in the string. This method returns the first position it finds the desired character in. There are also functions to return all the occurrences of a character from within a particular string.

14.2.3 Comparing Strings

There are also functions in programming languages that can be used to compare strings. Normally these methods compare a specified string with a source string, and then indicate whether the query precedes, follows, or appears in the same position in the sort order as the source string. The results of these comparisons are given below.

- If the value is less than zero, it means that the query string precedes the source value.

- If the value is greater than zero, it means that the query string follows the source value.

- If the value is equal to zero, then the query string has the same position in the sort order as the source value.

Below is an example that showcases the 'compareTo' method available in Java.

```java
public class Demo {
    public static void main(String args[]) {
        // Defining the string
        String str="Hello";
        System.out.println("The output is  " + str.compareTo("Hello"));
    }
}
```

In this sample, since both the strings are the same, a value of 0 will be returned. This is just one of many functions available for strings. Each programming language usually has a wide variety of functions and methods that can be used on strings.

15. Making Decisions in Programs

In almost every program there is a need to make decisions, and all programming languages provide a wide variety of statements specifically for decision making. At the heart of every decision-making statement is a condition. A condition is merely a yes/no question, such as "is the variable equal to 3?" or "is the variable a number?" The condition is evaluated, and depending on the result, a set of statements will be executed. Let's look at some of the most common forms of decision-making statements available.

15.1 The If Statement

This is the most basic form of decision making. In an 'if' statement, we have a condition which gets evaluated. Then if the condition evaluates to 'True', a set of statements will be executed. Below is a diagram that illustrates this process.

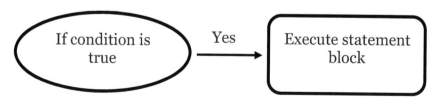

The most general syntax of the 'if' statement is given below:

```
if(condition)
{
//Execute code
}
```

Below is a sample of the 'if' statement in C#:

```
int i=3;
if(i==3)
Console.WriteLine("The value of i is " + i);
```

In this code sample we define a variable 'i' and assign a value of 3 to it. Then we use the 'if' statement to check the value of 'i'. If the value is equal to 3, the program will display the specified text in the console.

15.2 The If-Else Statement

The 'if-else' statement is similar to the standard 'if' statement, except it adds an additional option to execute a statement if the condition evaluates to 'False'. So again we start with a condition that is evaluated. Then if the condition evaluates to 'True', a set of statements will be executed. If the condition does not evaluate to 'True', a different set of statements are executed. Below is a diagram that illustrates this process.

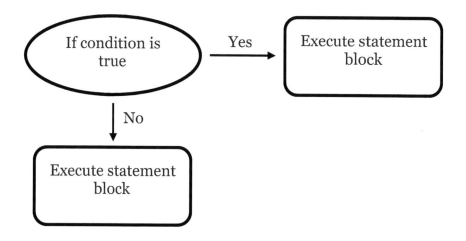

The most general syntax of the 'if-else' statement is given below:

```
if(condition)
{
//Execute code
}
else
{
//Execute code
}
```

Below is a sample of the 'if-else' statement in C#:

```
int i=4;
if(i==3)
Console.WriteLine("The value of i is " + i);
else
Console.WriteLine("The value of i is not equal to 3");
```

In this code sample we define a variable 'i' and assign a value of 4 to it. Then we use the 'if' statement to check the value of 'i'. If the value is equal to 3, the program will display the specified text in the console. Due to the 'else' statement the program will display an alternate text if the value is not equal to 3.

15.3 The Switch Statement

The 'switch' statement goes one step further than the 'if-else' statement and allows us to evaluate multiple conditions at a time, and then execute a statement that corresponds to each condition's outcome. So again we start with a condition that is evaluated. Then if the condition evaluates to 'True', a set of statements will be executed. If the condition does not evaluate to 'True', the program moves on to the next condition. This process is repeated for all conditions that we declare. If the program reaches the last condition and it also does not evaluate to 'True', a default statement can be executed. Below is a diagram that illustrates this process.

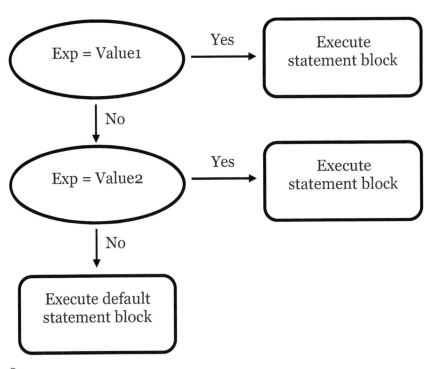

The most general syntax of the 'switch' statement is given below:

```
switch(expression)
{
  case constant-expression  :
    statement(s);
    break;
  case constant-expression  :
    statement(s);
    break;
  default :
  statement(s);
}
```

Below is a sample of the 'switch' statement in C#:

```
int i=4;
switch (i)
{
    case 1: Console.WriteLine("The value of i is 1");
    break;

    case 2: Console.WriteLine("The value of i is 2");
    break;

    case 3: Console.WriteLine("The value of i is 3");
    break;

    case 4: Console.WriteLine("The value of i is 4");
    break;

    default: Console.WriteLine("The value of i is unknown");
    break;
}
```

In this code sample we define a variable 'i' and assign a value of 4 to it. Then we use the 'switch' statement to evaluate the value of 'i'. Each case statement is then defined for the different possible values of 'i'. Finally we also define a default statement that gets executed if none of the case statements match the desired expression.

15.4 Nesting Statements

It is also possible to nest multiple decision-making statements within one another. An example would be placing one 'if' statement inside a second 'if' statement. So if the condition of the first 'if' statement evaluates to true, instead of a code statement being executed, the second 'if' statement is run.

There are multiple combinations of statements that can be used, and all of the decision-making statements we've discussed so far can be combined with one another. Care should however be taken when using nested statements. The more statements that are combined, the more complex the program becomes and the more difficult it is to keep track of the conditions being evaluated. An example of nested statements in C# is shown below.

```
int i=4;
    if (i > 0)
    {
    if (i == 4)
    {
    Console.WriteLine("The value is 4");
    }
}
```

16. Iterative Programming

Iterative programming refers to the process of executing a set of code statements a certain number of times. There are a variety of uses for iteration, such as stepping through a set of data records. To illustrate, imagine we have a set of data records (as shown below) stored in our program and want to display the ID and Name of each.

ID	Name
1	Mark
2	John
3	James

We would use an iterative loop statement to move through the data records and then display them accordingly. The first part of this process is to determine the number of iterations required. If we have three records, our iteration statements would repeat three times. The next part of the process is the iteration statements themselves. Let's look at some of the common iterative statements that are available across most programming languages.

16.1 The 'While' Iterative Loop

This loop statement starts by evaluating a particular condition. If the condition is 'True' then a set of statements is executed. The statements will be executed for as long as the condition evaluates to 'True'. Below is a diagram that illustrates this process.

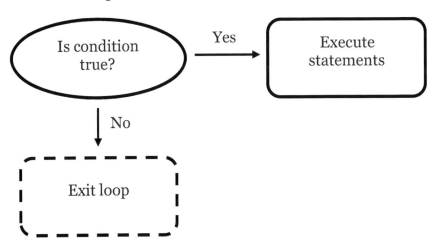

The most general syntax of the 'while' statement is given below:

```
While(condition)
{
//execute code
}
```

Below is a sample of the 'while' loop statement in Java:

```
int i=0;
    while(i<4)
    {
    System.out.println("The value of i is "+ i);
    i++;
}
```

In this sample program we define a variable 'i' and assign an initial value of 0 to it. Then we use the 'while' loop to evaluate the value of 'i'. As long as the value of 'i' is less than 4, the code statement in the 'while' code block will execute. The code block displays the value of 'i' and also increments the value of 'i'.

16.2 The 'Do-While' Iterative Loop

This loop statement is similar to the 'while' loop statement. The main difference between the two is that the 'do-while' loop evaluates the condition only after the code block is executed. The statements will then be executed for as long as the condition evaluates to 'True'. This means that we are always guaranteed that the code block will be executed at least once.

The most general syntax of the 'do-while' statement is given below:

```
do
{
//execute code
}
While(condition);
```

Below is a sample of the 'do-while' loop statement in Java:

```
do
    {
    System.out.println("The value of i is "+ i);
    i++;
    }
while(i<4);
```

In this sample program we start with the 'do' keyword to indicate that this is the beginning of the 'do-while' loop statement. Then we have the statement block which displays the value of 'i' and also increments the value of 'i'. Finally we have the 'while' statement that evaluates the value of 'i'. If the value of 'i' is less than 4, the program will loop from the beginning.

In both the 'while' and 'do-while' statements it is important to ensure that the condition can evaluate to 'False' at some point in the program. If it does not, the program will run indefinitely. For instance, in our code sample we increment the value of 'i' so it will eventually equal and exceed the value of 4.

16.3 The 'For' Iterative Loop

The 'for' loop statement can also be used to iterate through a set of statements. What makes this loop statement different from the preceding statements is that it compresses all the required parts into a single statement. This makes it much more compact than the other loops.

The 'for' statement consists of three main sections. The first is where we 'initialize' the variable and assign a value to it. The second is the 'condition' that needs to be evaluated. And lastly we 'increment' the value of the variable. Below is the syntax for the 'for' statement that illustrates this.

```
for(initialization;condition;incrementer)
{
//execute code
}
```

A diagram representing the 'for' loop process is shown below.

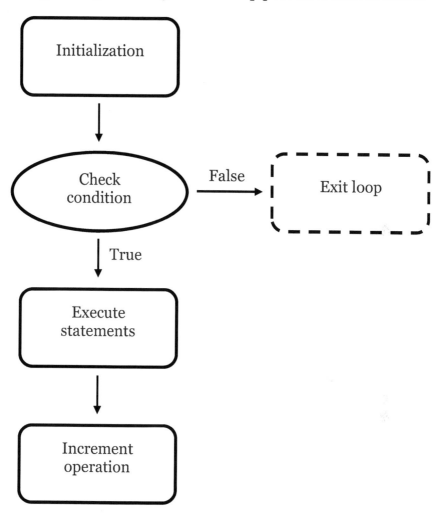

Below is a sample of the 'for' loop statement in Java:

```java
for(int i=0;i<4;i++)
{
    System.out.println("The value of i is "+ i);
}
```

In the above code sample we start with the 'for' statement and its three main components. First we initialize the variable 'i' and assign a value of 0 to it. We then state the condition for this loop. The condition tests whether the value of 'i' is less than 4. Thirdly we increment the value of 'i'. All of this is followed by the statement that gets executed based on the condition testing 'True".

16.4 Nesting Iterative Statements

The same principles used in nesting decision making statements, can be applied when nesting iterative statements. An example here would be placing a 'while' statement inside a 'for' statement. Again there are multiple combinations of statements that can be used, and all of the iterative statements we've discussed so far can be combined with one another. An example of nested iterative statements in C# is shown below.

```
for(int i=0;i<3;i++)
    {
      System.out.println("The value of i is "+ i);
      int j=0;
      while(j<3)
      {
        System.out.println("The value of j is "+ j);
        j++;
      }
    }
```

In this code sample we use a 'for' loop as the outer iterative statement, and a 'while' loop as the inner iterative statement. So for each iteration of the 'for' loop statement, the code block will run that includes the 'while' loop statement.

The 'while' loop will then go through its iterations, before exiting and returning to the 'for' loop. As can be seen here, care should definitely be taken when using nested iterative statements.

17. Logical Grouping of Code

Every program should be created with a specific purpose and a set of key requirements. As an example, if we intended to build an e-commerce application, we could come up with the following requirements:

- Have an inventory maintained for products

- Have products posted online for purchase

- Enroll and maintain customer data

- Allow customers to buy products

- Generate invoices

- Track payments

- Generate reports

So here we have our high-level requirements. If we move onto the design stage of the application, we could develop these requirements further by creating sub-requirements and even sub-sub-requirements. It is however easy to start losing focus of our primary goals as the program becomes larger and more complex. In these cases, we should consider breaking a program into logical pieces of code by using the available structures in a programming language.

Let's continue with our example by exploratory the 'Enroll and maintain customer data' requirement we mentioned above. By examining this requirement, we could break it down further into the following sub-requirements:

- Get Customer Data

- Add a new customer

- Edit details of the customer

- Delete existing customer details

- Generate reports on customer data

Instead of combining all of these sub-requirements in one code block, we should ideally segregate and group the code for each of these items. One of the most common practices is to develop methods or modules to segregate the code. In our example, we can define the following modules:

```
Input_customer_data()
  {
  //Enter code here
  }
Add_new_customer()
  {
  //Enter code here
  }
Edit_customer_data()
  {
  //Enter code here
  }
Delete_customer_data()
  {
  //Enter code here
  }
```

```
Generate_reports
    {
    //Enter code here
    }
```

Now we have five separate modules for our 'Enroll and maintain customer data' requirement. Each method will then have the necessary code to perform the functionality required for each sub-requirement. These methods can also be called from other modules, making the program much more efficient. Some other benefits of modularizing your code in this way are given below:

- Easy Maintenance – Since each section of code has a defined purpose, it becomes easier to modify the program at a later point in time. Instead of searching through thousands of lines of code to find the correct statement, you simply have to search through the various modules. This way there's also less of a chance to break the entire application when trying to modify one particular section.

- Easy Readability – It becomes considerably easier to "read" and understand a program when it's divided into blocks of code, rather than one large chunk of code.

- Code Reusability - This is a big selling point. Since the code is separated into modules that can be called at any point in time, you don't need to write the same piece of code over and over again.

17.1 Using Namespaces

Normally it's not only requirements that are broken down and written in modules, but also recurring functions. If a particular functionality needs to be written and used across several sections of an application, common practice is to write the code into a module and share it across the application.

For example, the process of retrieving data can be a common task that is required numerous times in an application. In our example above, we would need to retrieve data for both customers and products. We could then create a method called 'Input_data' that can be used for both the customer requirements and product requirements.

Since this method will be used across multiple requirements, we would need some way to distinguish it from the other code. We can do this at the top level, by making use of classes or even specific structures provided in programming languages. C#, for instance, allows for the use of something known as 'namespaces'. This can be used specifically to segregate functionality which is common across multiple modules.

Let's look at an example using our method called 'Input_data'.

```
using System;

// One namespace
namespace NameA{
   public class ClassA
   {
   public void FunctionA(){
      Console.WriteLine("This is namespace A");
   }
   }
}
```

```
// Second namespace
namespace NameB{
   public class ClassB
   {
      public void FunctionA()
      {
         Console.WriteLine("This is namespace B");
      }
   }
}
```

With the above program we are defining two namespaces, the one being 'NameA' and the other 'NameB'. Each namespace has a class defined and the same function defined. We can call each function via the namespace through the main calling program.

17.2 Anonymous Code Blocks

There are times when it might be preferred to limit the scope of a variable and use a code block only once. Most programming languages have the ability to define code blocks in a way that they cannot be used anywhere else. Below is an example of how this looks in C#.

```
void function()
{
 {
  int i = 0;
  i = i + 1;
 }
 {
  int k = 0;
  k = k + 1;
 }}
```

18. What Are Functions?

In the previous chapter, we looked at how we can use methods to segregate code into logical groupings. Well, these methods are also referred to as 'functions'. A function is simply a named section of code that performs a specific operation or task. We can write our own functions as we did in the previous chapter, or we can choose from a library of prewritten functions. Most programming languages come with built-in functions, but libraries can also be imported.

In this chapter we will look at the basic semantics of functions and how they can be used. Their application is similar across multiple programming languages, so our discussion doesn't need to focus on a specific language. We will start by looking at the definition of a function. The syntax is defined below.

```
FunctionName()
{
//code block
}
```

A function will have a function name, which is usually linked to the type of functionality that is carried out by the function. In a previous example, our function was used to import information from different sources. The name given to the function could then be 'Input_data()'.

Inside the brackets of the function, we have our code block that will be executed. This is the code that performs the necessary functionality. These are the basics of functions. Other intricacies to functions are concepts such as 'input parameters', 'returns values' and 'visibility'. Let's look at these aspects in more detail.

18.1 Input Parameters

There are instances when we might need to pass data to a function. Certain functions require data in order to perform their tasks properly. One of the simplest examples of this would be a function that adds two numbers together. The function requires the data of the two numbers it will be using. This can be done by passing the numbers to the function as parameters. Let's look at an example of this.

```
Add(int i,int j)
{
int k=i+j;
}
```

In the above sample code, we start by creating a function with a name of 'Add'. This function takes in two parameters of 'i' and 'j', and each parameter is a number, which is of the type 'integer'. The code block section of the function then adds these numbers together. When working with functions, we can pass a variety of parameters to a function. These parameters can be passed in the main program when the module is called. This can be done in the following way:

```
Add(2,3);
```

Here, the values of 2 and 3 are passed to the 'Add' method. The 'i' parameter will receive the value of 2, and the 'j' parameter will receive the value of 3.

18.2 Returning Values

Apart from taking in parameters, we can also use a function to return values to the calling program. Let's look at an example of this.

```
int Add(int i,int j)
{
int k=i+j;
return k;
}
```

In the above sample code, we start by creating a function with a name of 'Add'. This time, there is an additional keyword in front of the 'Add()' function. This is a data type that specifies what the type of value will be that is returned by the function. The function itself takes in two parameters of 'i' and 'j'. Each parameter is a number, which is of the type 'integer'. The code block section of the function then adds these numbers together, and also returns the resultant number. This time around, when we call the module in the main program, it will look the following way:

```
int out;
out=Add(2,3);
```

Here we are specifying that another variable should be defined that is of the type 'integer'. This variable will accept the return value sent by the 'Add' method.

When using return types you need to ensure the following:

- First. If you specify that the method returns a value by adding the prefix to the name, you need to return a value in the function code block.

- Second. The main calling program should have the facility to take the result from the function. And the return type accepted by the calling program should be the same as the return type specified by the function.

18.3 Visibility

Most programming languages allow us to change who is able to view and access a function. It is a core aspect of writing object-oriented programs. Functions (or methods) are normally contained within classes, which are used as the encapsulating entity. It is within the class that we define the visibility of a function. In C# it is done through using a class modifier. Class modifiers can be used to define the visibility of properties and methods in a class. Below are the various modifiers available.

- Private – With a private class, the properties and methods are only available to the class itself.

- Protected – With a protected class, the properties and methods are available to the class itself and any subclasses derived from that class.

- Public – With a public class, the properties and methods are available to all classes. So any program will have access to the methods within the class.

Let's look at an example of how a public class can be defined in C#.

```
class Program
{
public void Display()
    {
//Enter code here
    }
}
```

Here we have a class called 'Program', which has the method called 'Display'. Notice that it has been assigned a modifier of 'public'. This means that any other class can also call this method within the program. Let's look at the same program, but this time with a different access modifier.

```
class Program
{
public void Display()
    {
//Enter code here
    }
}
```

This time we have defined the access modifier as 'private'. This means that the 'Display' method cannot be used anywhere else outside of this class. Best practice in programming is implementing the principle of 'least privilege'. This means to assign the lowest level of access necessary to a function. If a function doesn't need to be accessed outside of its class, it should be defined as private.

19. Taking Input

Most programs will need to take some form of input from the user, in order for it to be processed by the functions we discussed earlier. The way in which input is taken by the program, will differ depending on the type of program we created. A web application, for instance, would take input differently compared to a console based script. Let's look at the different ways input can be processed, depending on the type of program being developed.

19.1 Console Based Applications

So let's start simple, with console-based applications. There are different ways in which input can be taken here. One of the most common methods is when the program is being executed. Most programming languages have the facility to accept input data when the program is being run for the first time. This input data is then accepted by the main code block of the program. Let's look at an example of how this is done in Java.

```
public class Program {
        public static void main(String[] args) {
        // Code block
    }
  }
```

In the above program, we first have our definition of the class. In the class we have the main block program; this is the entry point for the program. The main method then accepts an argument named 'args', which is an array of strings. When we call the main program, we can do it in the following way by adding a value:

```
Program One Two
```

The value of 'One' and 'Two' will now be passed to the program. If we wanted to see what values are being passed to the main program, we can output them back to the screen as shown in the code snippet below. Here we have our main program, but this time we are using a 'for' loop to go through all the values of the array and print them to the screen.

```java
public class Program {
    public static void main(String[] args) {
        for (String s: args) {
        System.out.println(s);
      }
    }
}
```

Another way we can input values in a console based application is by using the input streams that are accepted by the programming language. An example of this in Java is shown below, by using the following method:

```java
System.console().readLine();
```

This method can be used to read a line of text from the console. So the user will enter the text in the console and this can be then read by the main program.

19.2 Web Based Applications

Next we will look at the most common type of application out there, and that is web-based applications. When a web application requests input, it normally presents the user with a form to fill in. The data in the form is then read by the application and stored accordingly. Below is a snapshot of a simple HTML form that could be found on many HTML websites. HTML was the first language that was used to accept data.

If you look at the HTML form, you will notice that it has two input fields. One is for a first name and one is for a last name. We also have a 'Submit' button that transfers the data to our program to be processed. The program that is linked to this form would look something like this:

```
<!DOCTYPE html>
<html>
<body>

<form action="/action_page.php">
  First name:<br>
  <input type="text" name="firstname">
  <br>
  Last name:<br>
  <input type="text" name="lastname">
```

```
<br><br>
<input type="submit" value="Submit">
</form>

</body>
</html>
```

This is an HTML code page, which is used to generate the form. Each element in the form is generated via HTML code. Then we have a JavaScript program that is used to process the data on the front end. The JavaScript code can be used to verify that the data entered in the input form is correct, before it can be sent to the main program. This is an important step in order to minimize errors in the data.

For instance, the JavaScript code would need to detect if a user attempts to submit a blank value, and then prompt them to enter the data correctly. There are numerous aspects that could be important to check before data is sent back to the main program. Another example would be if we needed the user to enter their email address. The email ID should ideally contain the '@' symbol, which the JavaScript code can check for. So patterns can also be used to verify the data, before sending it back to the main program.

19.3 Taking in Data from Files

There are instances where it might be necessary to retrieve data from files. Programming languages have many file input and output classes that can be used to read data from files. Let's take an example from C#. There are a number of ways we can interact with files in this programming language. Let's look at an example code snippet.

```
static void Main(string[] args)
{
        // Opening the file in read only mode
        StreamReader src = new
StreamReader(@"G:\newHello.html");

        // Displaying the first line of the file
        Console.WriteLine(src.ReadLine());
}
```

Don't worry too much about the underlying code statements used in the program. In a nutshell, this is what the program does. It first uses a C# class called 'StreamReader' to open a file called 'newHello.html'. Then the same class is used to read the contents of the file, one line at a time.

Sometimes the data within files can follow a certain structure. This is true when you have XML or JSON structured files. Programming languages have separate ways of dealing with these files. Since these files have a definite structure, the programming language makes it easy to read the file in that defined structure.

As a final note, always be careful in the way you handle input data. Remember to always validate the data, because if the wrong type of data is entered in the program, it could lead to the wrong output or cause the entire program to become unstable.

20. Sending Output

Now that we've looked at taking input in our previous chapter, we will look at the opposite process of sending output from a program. The way in which output is given by the program, will differ depending on the type of program we created. So again, let's look at the different ways output can be processed, depending on the type of program being developed.

20.1 Console Based Applications

We will start again with the simplest form, that being console based applications. Most programming languages have methods that can be used to write data to the console. This process is very important when it comes to testing the behavior of a program and making sure it operates as intended. Let's look at an example of how this is done in C#.

```
static void Main(string[] args)
{
Console.Write("Hello World");
}
```

The above program is very simple and uses the 'Console' class that is available in C#. This class contains a method called

'Write', which then writes the string 'Hello' to the console. The 'Console' class also has the facility to write data to different lines using the 'WriteLine' method. Let's look at a code snippet which will write 'Hello' on the first line and 'World' now on a second line.

```
static void Main(string[] args)
{
Console.WriteLine("Hello");
Console.WriteLine("World");
}
```

20.2 Web Based Applications

When it comes to HTML based applications, we've already seen how to input data with an input form. But certain programming languages, such as C# and Java, have added functionality to dynamically generate output that can be sent to the user. There are web-based frameworks which are available in these programming languages specifically designed for this purpose. For example, in C# we can use the code snippet below to send 'Hello World' to the user whenever they request a particular webpage.

```
html xmlns="http://www.w3.org/1999/xhtml">
<head runat="server">
  <title></title>
</head>
<body>
  <form id="form1" runat="server">
    <% Response.Write("Hello World"); %>
    <div>
    </div>
  </form>
</body>
</html>
```

Don't worry too much about the underlying code. What is important to note here is the line 'Response.Write("Hello World")'. 'Response' is a special class in C# that can be used to write data back to the webpage requested by the user. In our example the string 'Hello World' will be displayed on the webpage. This functionality extends far beyond lines of text. We can generate entire HTML pages and send it back to the user.

20.3 Sending Data Output to Files

In the same way that data can be read from files, we can have data written back to files. Programming languages have many file input and output classes that can be used to write data to files. Let's take an example from C#. There are a number of ways we can interact with files in this programming language. Let's look at an example code snippet used to write data to a file.

```
static void Main(string[] args)
    {

        // Opening the file in append mode
        StreamWriter src = new
StreamWriter(@"G:\newHello.html");

        // Writing contents to the file
        src.WriteLine("Hello World");
}
```

Again don't worry too much about the underlying contents of the program. In a nutshell, the program uses a C# class called 'StreamWriter' to open a file called 'newHello.html'. Then the same class is used to write the line 'Hello World' to the file.

113

21. What Is Functional Programming?

Functional programming is computing paradigm or way of thinking. It focusses on pure functions and avoids changing-state and mutable data. To explain all of this, let's have a look at the key aspects of functional programming.

21.1 Immutability

The first key aspect is that functional programming is considered to be immutable. An immutable object's state cannot be changed after it is created. To illustrate, imagine we defined a function in a program with a specific purpose. If the state of the output is the same whenever the input is the same, then that function follows the functional programming paradigm. If the function changes the state of data and gives a different output for the same input, then that function does not follow the functional programming paradigm.

21.2 No Side Effects

Another important aspect of functional programming is not having side effects. So what exactly is a side effect? It is when a function does something that is outside the boundaries of what it is supposed to do.

Let's say we defines a function called 'GetStudentData', which takes in a student ID and then gives the student name as the result. If this function is defined properly, the student name should always be the same for the same student ID. But if the function does further internal processing, like modifying the student ID based on other parameters before retrieving the student name, then this could result in a different output. This is an undesired side effect of the function.

21.3 Expression Based

Another trait of functional programming is that a functional program deals more with expressions than statements. To illustrate, let's look at a simple statement based program.

```
string result;
if(value>0)
result ="Greater than 0"
else
result="Less than 0"
```

In the above program we define a variable called 'result', which is a string data type. Then we state a condition for the variable called 'value'. We assign a string to the variable 'result' depending on whether the value is greater or less than 0. Now let's look at the same piece of code, but this time using expressions.

```
var result=value>0?"positive":"negative"
```

So here we are implementing the same logic, but programming languages have expressions available that can achieve the same result.

In our example we have a ternary expression, which accomplishes the same as the set of statements defined earlier. One advantage of using expressions is that the code becomes more concise and manageable.

21.4 Higher-Order Functions

Next we'll look at the concept of higher-order functions. These are functions that can either take other functions as arguments or return them as results. In functional programming, functions are deemed as first class citizens. This means that they are allowed to appear anywhere in the code. They can also be used as parameters to other functions. For example, the Python code below shows that we can define functions that call other functions.

```
def a(x)
return x+5
def b(c,x)
return c(x)*2
print(b(a,30))
```

Probably the most common place you might have seen this is when generating Fibonacci numbers. The code below is used to generate the 10 Fibonacci numbers using complete functional programming in PHP.

```
function fib(int $n) : int {
    return ($n === 0 || $n === 1) ? $n : fib($n - 1) + fib($n - 2);
}
for ($i = 0; $i <= 10; $i++) echo fib($i) . PHP_EOL;
```

21.5 Pure Functions

A major selling point for functional programming is having pure functions. These are small functions that have been built for a specific purpose. To elaborate, assume we wanted to decide if a value is less than or greater than 0. We could define the function as shown below.

```
bool decide(int value)
{
string result;
if(value>0)
result ="Greater than 0"
else
result="Less than 0"
return result
}
```

We have seen a similar piece of code earlier. Here we pass the value to the function and then return the desired result. Now we could very well also define two pure functions instead by splitting up the above functionality. One function would determine if the value was greater than 0 and the other function would determine if the value was less than 0. This program would look something like this:

```
bool decidegreater(int value)
{
if(value>0) return true else return false;
}
bool decideless(int value)
{
if(value<0) return true else return false;
}
```

22. What Is Object Oriented Programming?

Object oriented programming is the most common programming paradigm used in the world today. One of the earliest languages, C++, was made to incorporate this paradigm. The foundation of object-oriented programming is the use of classes. A class is defined as an entity representation, which can have properties and methods.

To get a better idea of classes, imagine you are working on an e-commerce application. As part of the requirements you need to manage the orders. So each order would classify as an entity. Now you need some way to represent that entity in a programming language. This can be done by using classes, and can be represented as shown below.

```
class Orders
{
//code
}
```

Here, 'Orders' is the name given to the class. The orders will have information pertaining to them, such as the order ID and description. In a class, these can be represented by properties of the class. These properties can then be used to hold information about the object.

We can incorporate properties for an order ID and description into our previous example, which will now look as follows:

```
class Orders
{
int orderID;
string orderDesc;
}
```

Obviously if an entity has data, there need to be actions to act upon that data. For this purpose classes can have methods which are used to work on data. To continue our example, let's say we wanted to display the order ID and description. We would then change our program as follows:

```
class Orders
{
int orderID;
string orderDesc;
void Display()
{
//Code to display the Order ID and description
}
}
```

Now we have a method in the 'Orders' class, which is used to display the order ID and description. There are many more aspects to object-oriented programming and uses for classes. We will now look at those in greater detail.

22.1 Encapsulation

This refers to the encapsulation or bundling of data and methods into classes. An integral part of this mechanism is the

120

visibility of this data in the class. There are situations where we don't want to directly allow other code to access the data defined in the class. In such cases, we only want data to be accessed via methods defined in the class. There are different levels of visibility which are defined by class modifiers. There are:

- Private – With private, the properties and methods are only available to the class itself.

- Protected - With protected, the properties and methods are available to the class itself and subclasses derived from that class.

- Public - With public, the properties and methods are available to all classes.

An example of how data can be encapsulated in a C# class is shown below. In this code we define the student ID and the student Name as private members so that they cannot be accessed directly. If any other code wants to see the ID and name values, they can call the 'Display' method of the class.

```
    class Student
{
    // The members of the class
  private int studentID;
  private string studentName;
    // Declaring a member function
  public void Display()
  {
    Console.WriteLine("The ID of the student is " + studentID);
    Console.WriteLine("The name of the student is " +
studentName);
  }
}
```

22.2 Inheritance

The next concept we will look at is inheritance. This simply means that we can define a class to inherit the properties and methods of another class. The main advantage of this is, not having to define the properties and methods again when defining a new class.

Imagine we have a class named 'Person', which has a property called 'Name' and a method called 'Display'. By way of inheritance we can define a new class named 'Student' and have it inherit the property and method of the 'Person' class. The Student class could then define its own additional members if required. Let's look at a code snippet of this in C#.

```
// Defining the base class
class Person
{
   public string Name;
}

class Student:Person
{
   public int ID;

   // Declaring a member function
   public void Display()
   {
// Code
   }
};
```

With the above program we define a class called 'Person', which has one member called 'Name'. This is normally known as the base class. A base class is the primary class from which a second class inherits its data. We then use inheritance to define the 'Student' class, which will get the properties and methods of the 'Person' class. Notice that we now define another property called 'ID'. Lastly in the 'Display' function, note that we can use the 'Name' property without the need for defining it in the 'Student' class again.

22.3 Polymorphism

The last concept we will discuss is polymorphism. This refers to a situation where a base class and derived class can have the same function with the same name. The function that gets called in the program, depends on the type of class from which the function gets called. Let's look at a simple example of this using C#.

```
    class Person
{
    public int ID;
    public void Display()
    {
// Write Code here

    }
};

class Student:Person {
    public new void Display()
    {
//Code here
    }
};

    class Program
    {
```

```
    // The main function
    static void Main(string[] args)
    {
        Student stud1=new Student();
        stud1.ID = 1;
        stud1.Display();

        Person per1=new Person();
        per1.ID = 2;
        per1.Display();

    }
  }
}
```

Don't worry too much about the details of the program. The main aspects to take note of are that there are two classes, the one being 'Person' and the other being 'Student'. Both classes define the same method called 'Display', but when we use either class, the method called depends on the type of class being used.

23. What Are Client Server Applications?

O ne of the most important decisions to make when designing an application, is whether it will be a client-server application or a web-based application. In this chapter we will look at client-server applications in greater detail, with web programming covered in the next chapter.

A client-server application, in its simplest form, will consist of two components. The first is the server component. This is usually a rather powerful computer that processes network traffic. This is where all of the business and program logic is hosted. The second component is the client portion, which is usually a standard PC or workstation. This is where the client program will be installed that interacts with the server component. The below diagram shows this representation.

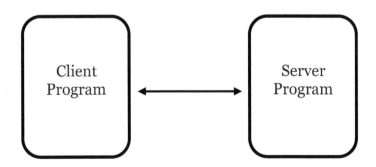

Sometimes it is beneficial to design client-server applications. One of the biggest design considerations is the amount of data flow between the client and server. Client-server applications can handle a significant amount of data compared web applications, where web applications are limited by bandwidth and connection quality. Client-server applications are particularly popular to use for enterprise resourcing.

There are a number of disadvantages to these applications as well. Since the client program is designed to contain a lot of functionality, it sometimes becomes a little bulky and difficult to maintain. The client program also needs to be installed for every user, as well as updated for every user with every single revision.

Nevertheless, programming languages have been created with the ability to design and work with client-based applications. Using a language like C#, you can develop simple console based applications or even forms-based applications. These programs can also make use of underlying libraries to interact with networking components and database components. Below is a snapshot for a very simple forms-based application developed in C#.

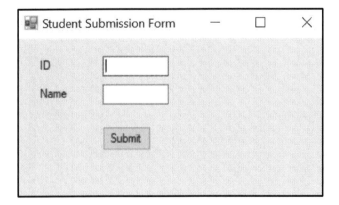

This form is extremely simple and only has input for an ID and name, along with a submission button. When the button is pressed, the details of the ID and the name can be sent for further processing. Normally when you develop such forms-based applications, you also get a lot of skeleton code that comes along with it. For example, for the above form in C# you would already have the below skeleton code.

```
using System;

using System.Windows.Forms;

namespace WindowsFormsApp1
{
    public partial class Form1 : Form
    {
        public Form1()
        {
            InitializeComponent();
        }

        private void label2_Click(object sender, EventArgs e)
        {

        }

        private void Form1_Load(object sender, EventArgs e)
        {

        }
    }
}
```

Again, there's no need to delve into the detail of the above code. What is important to understand is that there are 'events' code put in place for the different controls in the form.

A program type that could be considered a client-server application, is actually an Integrated Development Environment such as Visual Studio. Since it has the ability to connect to various resources such as Microsoft SQL Server on certain ports and retrieve data, it can be considered a client-server application.

If you decide to opt for a client-server application, it's important to ensure that the programming language you intend to use has the capability to create these applications. Most of the programming languages such as C++, C#, Python and Java support client-server applications.

24. What Is Web Programming?

Now that we've discussed client-server applications in the previous chapter, we will look at web-based applications next. This is probably the most common type of program today, especially since the increased availability of internet access around the world.

A web-based application is a program that has been developed so that it can be accessed via a web browser, rather than existing on a client's workstation. A small part of the application could still be downloaded onto the user's system, however all of the processing is handled on an external server.

A big advantage of web-based applications is that the program can be accessed by a wide variety of web browsers, making it easy for users to access the program. This also means that it's not necessary to download or install any major software on the client's machine. As mentioned, most of the processing is done on the server side. This means the application won't slow down the user's system, if the system wouldn't normally be capable of running the program. Below is the simplest representation of a web-based application.

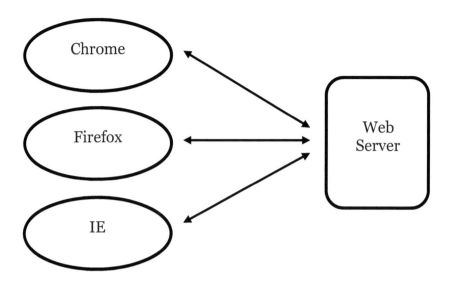

The underlying web server being used depends largely on the type of programming language adopted. Some of the most popular web serving software are given below.

- Apache Tomcat - This is an open source Java servlet container that functions as a web server. A Java servlet is a Java program that extends the capabilities of a server. With Java servlets you can generate dynamic web pages.

- NGINX - This is a popular web server that relies on an asynchronous event-driven architecture to help power its goal of handling massive concurrent sessions.

- Apache HTTP Server - This has been the most popular web server since 1996 and is still popular to date.

- IIS - This web server is used for hosting ASP.Net based applications.

- Node.js - This is a server-side JavaScript environment for network applications such as web servers.

Almost all programming languages support web-based programs. Each programming language has a different representation of the code that is used to generate web pages, but all languages allow for the dynamic generation of web pages. Below is an example of a web-based application in C#.

```
using System;

namespace WebApplication2
{
    public partial class WebForm1 : System.Web.UI.Page
    {
        protected void Page_Load(object sender, EventArgs e)
        {
            Response.Write("Welcome to the world of web
programming");
        }
    }
}
```

When we execute the code in the Visual Studio IDE, we would get the following output:

Once a program such as the one above has been developed, it needs to be hosted on a web server. The process involves transferring the files to the server in order to access the link from the web server.

Each programming language has a series of steps in order to transfer and port applications onto their respective web hosting platforms. For example, the following steps are generally followed when deploying a Java based application onto a Tomcat web server:

- Package the Java application into a .war file. This can be done via the Integrated Development Environment.

- Copy the .war file into the $CATALINA_HOME\webapps directory on the Tomcat web server.

- Restart the server. Whenever Tomcat is started, it will unpack the .war file it found in the \webapps directory and launch the application.

Some of the other various aspects that should be looked at when developing a web program are:

- Storage of data – It's important to maintain and manage the stored data, as it will be a central access point for users.

- Storing of user information – Sometimes to create a better user experience, some web programs might store user preferences. The purpose is for returning users to get the same experience they had when they visited the program earlier. This can be done by storing something known as cookies on the client computer or server.

- Design for performance – Since the web program would be used by multiple users, the program should be designed for maximum performance and efficiency. If the environment which hosts the program becomes unstable due to bad programming practices, it could affect all users who are accessing the application.

- Security – Since most web programs are designed to be used over the internet, the program must be designed and developed with security in mind. This is not only to protect the application from tampering, but the information that might be contained in its databases.

- Usage on different devices – These days, programs are not only accessed from computers, but also from mobile devices such as phones and tablets. So if a web application might be accessed from a phone, this should be taken into account when developing the program.

- Being careful with changes – Because a web program can be used by multiple users, care should be taken when making changes to the application. A change could potentially fix errors for some users, while creating problems for others.

25. Managing Data in a Program

Working with data is an integral part of programming. Data is used for processing, it's passed between components and modules within a program, and even passed between programs. But the most important aspect of data is its storage. In this chapter we will look at the various ways in which we can store data in a program.

25.1 Single Values

One of the simplest ways of storing data, is storing singular values as numbers or strings. In order to do this, we would define a variable of a particular data type that would be used to store the value. As an example, consider the C# code snippet below.

```
int i=5;
String str="Mark";
```

Here we have two definitions of data. The first definition is that of a number, which has a value of 5. This value is then stored in a variable called 'i'.

The next definition is that of a string "Mark". This is stored in a variable called 'str'. This is one of the simplest representations of data in a program. The data can be modified and used in other aspects of the program as well.

25.2 Data Array

There are times when single values might not be sufficient for your needs, and it would be necessary to store a set of values. The representation of this type of data is done via an array. Almost all programming languages have the capability of using arrays to store a contiguous set of values. Below is a code snippet in Java showing how an array can be declared and defined.

```
// Declaring the Array
int[] arr=new int[3];
// Defining the elements of the array
arr[0]=1; // The first element of the array
arr[1]=2; // The second element of the array
arr[2]=3; // The third element of the array
```

Here we are defining an array that can hold three values. We can then assign separate values to each part of the array. This array can be used across the span of the entire program at any point in time. Using arrays help negate setting up multiple variables and values for each. Programming languages allow arrays to be defined for multiple data types, including numbers and string.

25.3 Collections

This is a more advanced way of storing data, and is useful to store a collection of data. It's similar to an array, but more dynamic in nature. One limitation of an array is that you need to define the number of elements of the array beforehand. However in the case of a collection, you can define the elements of the array dynamically as you progress. Below is a code snippet in C# showing how an 'ArrayList' collection can be defined.

```
ArrayList ar = new ArrayList();
    // Adding elements to the array list
    ar.Add(1);
    ar.Add(2);
    ar.Add(3);
```

Here we first define an 'ArrayList', which is a special collection available in C#. Notice that when declaring the array list we don't need to define the number of array elements beforehand. We can simply add elements to the array list using the predefined methods available for that collection. So in the above scenario, we are using the 'Add' method to add data elements to the array list. There are different types of collections available in the various programming languages to meet the needs of almost any program.

25.4 Classes

Now we come to by far the most popular way to store data. Classes represent an encapsulation of data. With collections and arrays, we can only define one type of data element at a time. So let's say we want to store the ID and name of several customers. We would need to define two separate arrays or collections, one for the ID and the other for the name. However with classes we can group these two elements, and then create properties for each. Let's take an example from C# to illustrate.

```
Class Customer
{
int ID;
String Name;
}
```

In the above code segment, we define a class called 'Customer'. This class encapsulates two properties, one is called 'ID' and the other is called 'Name'. They both have their own corresponding data types. Now if we want to capture the data for a particular student, we would define an object for the class as shown below.

```
Customer customer1-new Customer();
customer1.ID=1;
customer1.Name=Mark;
```

You can also make use of a combination of classes and collections to define an entire collection of customer objects. So you can see that there are multiple ways to store data in a program. It all depends on the type of data you want to store and the way you want to access the data.

26. Storing Data in Files

In the previous chapter we looked at storing data in a program. After a program stops executing, the data in the program will be disposed of and will no longer be available. Hence there should be some way of making the data available even after the program terminates. This is where disk storage becomes important, and one of the ways of doing this is by storing data in files.

Almost all programming languages have the ability to store data in files. They provide a plethora of functions that can be used to read and write data to and from files. If we look at C# as an example, it has classes called 'Stream' classes that are used for this exact purpose. The diagrams below show the depiction of these streams.

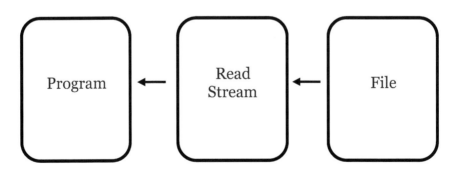

First we have the 'Read' stream. Here the program ensures that there is a stream that flows from the file on the hard disk to the program. Whenever a request is made from the program to read contents from a file, the stream reads the bytes of data from the file and then transfers it back to the program. An example of what a stream reader looks like in C# is given below.

```
StreamReader src = new StreamReader(@"G:\newHello.html");
// Displaying the first line of the file
Console.WriteLine(src.ReadLine());
```

In the above code snippet we first have the definition of the 'StreamReader' object. This is used to ensure that a stream is established to the file called 'newHello.html'. Then the 'ReadLine' method of the stream reader class is used to read a line from the file.

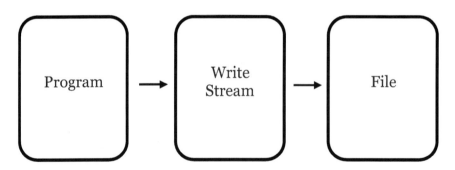

Similar to the 'Read' stream, we also have the 'Write' stream. When a request is made from the program to write contents to a file, the stream takes the data from the program and then writes the data to the file. An example of the stream writer class in C# is given below.

```
StreamWriter src = new StreamWriter(@"G:\newHello.html");
// Writing contents to the file
src.WriteLine("Hello World");
```

In the above code snippet we first have the definition of the 'StreamWriter' object. This is used to ensure that a stream is established to the file called 'newHello.html'. Next, the 'WriteLine' method of the stream writer class is used to write a line to the file

One point to note about the above streams is that the 'StreamReader' and 'StreamWriter' classes do the job of converting the strings to bytes and vice versa. Remember that in the end, the data in the file is stored as bytes. That is why we use these classes to convert our data. There are also classes that allow direct interaction with the file in bytes. In C# we use the 'FileStream' class for this purpose.

Obviously this adds another level of complexity to the program, but as you start developing more and more programs, classes like these will become easier to use. Below is an example of the 'FileStream' class in C#.

```
// Opening the file in read only mode
FileStream src = new
FileStream(@"G:\Hello.html",FileMode.Open, FileAccess.Read);
// Number of bytes in the file
int numBytes = (int)src.Length;
// This will be used to get the number of bytes read
int i = 0;
// Storing the bytes in an array
byte[] bytes = new byte[src.Length];
src.Read(bytes, i, numBytes);
string result = System.Text.Encoding.UTF8.GetString(bytes);
```

It's not necessary to fully understand the inner working of the above program, but in a nutshell it does the following. We open the file 'Hello.html' with the options 'FileMode.Open, FileAccess.Read' so that we can read from the file.

The variable 'bytes' is then used to store all the bytes that are read from the file. The function 'System.Text.Encoding.UTF8. GetString' is used to convert the list of bytes into a string.

Once you become more accustomed to working with files, it will become much easier to work with the various methods. Depending on the type of data you want to store, you should choose the type of file access that suits your needs best. If you are working with simple text files, then use the 'StreamReader' and 'StreamWriter' classes. If you are working with XML data and want to ensure the file size is as small as possible, then use the 'FileStream' class.

27. Storing Data in Databases

Apart from storing data in files, another popular way of storing data is in databases. There are a number of benefits when using a database over a file system. These are discussed next.

- Easy retrieval – Getting data from a database is simpler and easier than getting it from a file. If you wanted to get a certain aspect of data from a file, you would normally need to go through the entire file to search for the data. This is a lengthy process, especially if it is a large life. Databases, on the other hand, have special commands that can be issued to search for data. They also have specific techniques to speed up data retrieval.

- Storing large amounts of data – Databases are designed to store large amounts of data. Files normally have limitations on size based on the format and operating system used, but databases can support large amounts of data.

- Structured data – Databases allow you to structure your data in a proper way. So if you wanted to store all information pertaining to customers, you could have a separate table dedicated to customer data only.

- Having dependencies – Databases allow you to have relationships between data, such as a specific link between customers and orders.

Databases make use of tables in order to store data. For example, we could have a table called Customers that stores the following data:

CustomerID	CustomerName
1	Mark
2	Joe

In relational database systems 'CustomerID' and 'CustomerName' are referred to as the columns of the table, while the remaining values form the rows of the table. The following basic operations can be performed on tables:

- Select operation – This is used to select or retrieve a piece of data from a table. It is normally used as part of a query that retrieves data.

- Insert operation – This is used to put data into a table. So if we need to add a new customer to the table, we would use this operation.

- Update operation – This is used to update a particular data value in the table.

- Delete operation – This is used to delete a particular value from the table.

Some of the most popular database systems are given below.

- Oracle Database - This is a multi-model database management system produced and marketed by Oracle Corporation. It is the world's most popular database for running online transaction processing (OLTP), data warehousing (DW) and mixed database workloads (OLTP & DW).

- MySQL - This is an open-source relational database management system (RDBMS).

- Microsoft SQL Server - This is a relational database management system developed by Microsoft. As a database server, its primary function is storing and retrieving data as requested by other software applications. These applications may run either on the same computer or on another computer across a network.

- PostgreSQL - This is an object-relational database management system (ORDBMS) with an emphasis on extensibility and standards compliance.

- MongoDB - This is a free and open-source cross-platform document-oriented database program. It is classified as a NoSQL database program and uses JSON-like documents.

Almost all programming languages provide support for the various databases. When working with databases in any programming language there are a series of steps that should be followed. Let's look at these steps using C# as an example.

Step 1: Establishing a connection

The first and foremost step is to establish a connection to the database. Once a connection is established, we can continue to interact with the database. The C# code snippet below shows how to establish a connection to a database.

```
using(SqlConnection conn = new SqlConnection())
{
    conn.ConnectionString =
"Server=[server_name];Database=[database_name];Trusted_Conn
ection=true";
}
```

In the above example, we first use the 'SqlConnection' class in C# to create a new connection to the database. Each database connection is associated with a connection string. This string defines the necessary information that is required to establish a connection with the database. The connection string normally contains the server name where the database is hosted, as well as the database name.

Step 2: Creating a command object

This is used to express what type of operation we want to perform on the database. Whether we want data from a particular table or to put a record in a table, this is where we specify the operations mentioned earlier. Below is an example of a command object where we ask to retrieve a list of customers from the customer table.

```
SqlCommand command = new SqlCommand("SELECT * FROM
Customers", conn);
```

Step 3: Reading data

Once the data we want has been retrieved, we can use additional statements to read and process the data. For instance, if we retrieve multiple rows of data, we could use a statement like the one shown below to read the data one row at a time.

```
using (SqlDataReader reader = command.ExecuteReader())
{
    while (reader.Read())
    {
    //Read the data
    }
}
```

Step 4: Insert, delete or update statements

Other actions that can be performed on the data is to insert new data, or to update or delete existing data. Below is an example of inserting a new row into the customer table.

```
SqlCommand insertCommand = new SqlCommand("INSERT INTO
Customers (CustomerID, CustomerName) VALUES (1, 'John')",
conn);
```

Databases are by far the most popular storage method, and the available database options keep growing day by day. There are databases that are even completely serverless in concept. This means that the underlying server capacity doesn't need to be managed, only the data itself. An example is the DynamoDB database from Amazon Web Services.

If you are interested in learning more about databases and SQL, be sure to check out our beginners guide on the subject.

SQL

Programming Basics for Absolute Beginners

a FREE Kindle Version with Paperback

28. Data Exchange Formats

It is not uncommon for applications to exchange data with other applications in one form or another. Exchanging data within a program is quite simple, as we have seen with arrays, collections and classes. However when it comes to exchanging data between programs, there are a few specific aspects that need to be considered beforehand. These considerations can be summarized into the following questions:

- What type of data needs to be transferred?

- Does the destination program have the ability to understand the data being sent by the source program?

- Does the source program have the ability to transform the data into a format that the destination program can understand?

- What is the total amount of data being transferred?

- What is the size of each data item being transferred?

- Is the source program and destination program written in the same programming language?

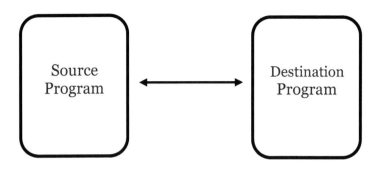

All of the above are key questions that should be answered when looking at data exchange. Let's take an example of a source program that needs to transfer a set of purchase orders to a destination program. The questions can then be applied to our example as follows:

- Are we sending a sequence of strings that contain the order data, or do we need to send the entire order information such as the order ID, order quantity etc. separately?

- How does the destination program know that we are sending order information? And how does it dissect and process the different pieces of order information?

- Does the source program have the capability of sending the order information in a way that it can be understood by the destination program?

- How many orders need to be sent between the source and destination program?

- What is the size of each purchase order that needs to be sent?

- The source program is written in .Net and the destination program is written in Java. Will the data exchange still work?

Over the years, numerous data exchange formats have been invented for sending information from one program to another. Let's look at some of the most popular.

28.1 XML

The most famous data exchange format over the years has been the XML markup language. The XML document contains the data to be transferred, and the XML language defines the structure of the document. Most programming languages have the capability, either built-in or as an add-on, to work with XML data.

For example, if we have a source program developed in .Net, there are libraries available for .Net that can construct XML documents. These XML documents would then be sent to the destination program. If the destination program is in Java, it would have its own libraries to dissect the XML documents.

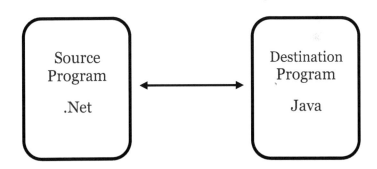

A sample XML document is given below.

```
<PurchaseOrder PurchaseOrderNumber="101">
 <Address Type="Shipping">
  <Name>Mark</Name>
  <Street>123 Street</Street>
```

```
</Address>
<Items>
  <Item Part="123">
    <ProductName>Shaver</ProductName>
    <Quantity>1</Quantity>
    <USPrice>18.95</USPrice>
  </Item>
</PurchaseOrder>
```

The XML document is similar to an HTML document which has tags. You might notice that the document is structured in a way that makes it easy to break into logical segments. So in our document above we have a purchase order, an address, an item, and the details of the item. We could also have multiple purchase orders in a single XML document.

28.2 JSON

JSON stands for JavaScript Object Notation, and is an extremely popular format for transmitting data between programs. With JSON objects are transmitted as simple key value pairs. An example of a JSON document is given below.

```
{
  "firstName": "Mark",
  "lastName": "Smith",
  "age": 27,
  "address": {
    "streetAddress": "1st Street",
    "city": "New York",
    "postalCode": "10021-31"
  },
  "phoneNumbers": [
    {
```

```
    "type": "home",
    "number": "312 555-1234"
  },
  {
    "type": "office",
    "number": "647 555-4567"
  },
  {
    "type": "mobile",
    "number": "124 456-7890"
  }
 ]
}
```

The JSON syntax is very similar to JavaScript. The JSON document is also structured in a way that makes it easy to break into logical segments. In the above JSON document we define a person with multiple attributes. There are single attributes, such as first name and last name. And then there are combined attributes, such as phone numbers.

28.3 YAML

This is known as 'Yet Another Markup Language' and is a human-readable data serialization language. It is commonly used for configuration files, but can also be used in many applications where data is stored or transmitted. An example of a YAML document is given below.

```
database:
  username: admin
  password: password
memcached:
  host: 10.0.0.101
```

```
workers:
 - host: 10.0.0.103
   port: 2301
 - host: 10.0.0.104
   port: 2302
```

In the above YAML document, we have a configuration file defined. This file contains information such as a database username and password, and host information for a Memcached solution.

Choosing a data exchange format is highly dependent on the languages you will be using. For example, JSON makes most sense when working with JavaScript. The type and size of the data being transferred will also play a big part in your decision. JSON is better for processing large data sets, but XML is better suited for sounds and images. In the end, unless you are forced by external web services to use a specific format, it might just come down to personal preference.

29. Error Handling

Every program is prone to errors, no matter how meticulous we might be. It is just impossible to test for every error condition and ensure that a program works flawlessly, especially when we consider that an unpredictable end user will be using the application. Hence we should always code in a way that tries to anticipate errors, and provides a way to resume the program if an unexpected error occurs. It's not a great user experience if the program terminates after an error.

In most programming languages there are ways for programs to intercept errors and handle them accordingly. These types of errors are known as exceptions, and programming languages have statements that are designed to catch these exceptions and deal with them accordingly.

For example, if we created a program that has to access a file on the local file system, the program should ideally first check for the existence of a file before proceeding ahead. But let's say that the user can proceed without selecting a file. The program will then throw an error when it tries to access the non-existent file. In such a case, the program should try to handle the error appropriately by requesting the user to select a file, rather than terminating the program.

Almost all programming languages have a system for catching exceptions. It is most commonly known as 'try' and 'catch' blocks. The code that is anticipated to cause an error would be placed in the 'try' block, while the code that is meant to execute in case of an error is placed in the 'catch' block.

Let's look at an example in C# to illustrate this concept. The code below is used to assign a value to an array variable. If we foresee that this code might cause an error, we could place it inside a 'try' block.

```
try
{
    i[3] = 3;
}
```

We could then declare the array as shown below. This is a legal statement and will pass the 'try' block.

```
int[] i = new int[2];
```

Alternatively we could declare the array as shown below. This code statement will cause an error. That is because the array is only designed to hold values up to an index value of 3, but we are trying to assign a value to the array index of 4.

```
int[] i = new int[4];
```

If we were to execute this code, we would get an error stating that the index is outside the bounds of the array, after which the program would exit. Hence we have to make provision for this error in our program. So in addition to the 'try' block, we would need to add a 'catch' block to our program. When an exception occurs in the program, the exception would then be passed to the 'catch' block. The code in the 'catch' block will then enable the program to proceed ahead without closing. By adding the 'catch' block, our program will look like this:

```
int[] i = new int[2];
try
{
    i[3] = 3;
}
catch(Exception ex)
{
        Console.WriteLine(ex.Message);
}
```

Our 'catch' block simply displays an error message, but the good part is that the code will still continue working as it should and not terminate abruptly.

Each programming language has pre-defined exceptions already built in to handle specific types of errors. This means we can use these classes to deal with common errors instead of writing our own from scratch. The table below shows the different types of exceptions defined in C#.

Exceptions in C#

Exception	Description
System.IO.IOException	This is used to handle I/O errors
System.IndexOutOfRange Exception	This is used to handle errors generated when a method refers to an array index out of range

Exception	Description
System.ArrayTypeMismatchException	This is used to handle errors generated when the array type is mismatched
System.NullReferenceException	This is used to handle errors generated from referencing a null object
System.DivideByZeroException	This is used to handle errors generated from dividing a dividend with zero
System.InvalidCastException	This is used to handle errors generated during typecasting
System.OutOfMemoryException	This is used to handle errors generated from insufficient free memory
System.StackOverflowException	This is used to handle errors generated from stack overflow

It's not necessary to go into depth into the different classes for exception handling. For our purposes, let's look at how our code can be written if we use a built-in class.

```
int[] i = new int[2];
try {
    i[3] = 3;
  }
catch (System.IndexOutOfRangeException ex) {
    Console.WriteLine(ex.Message);
}
```

By using one of these built-in classes, we would need to know the type of potential error we may get in order to use the correct class. But what if we don't know what type of error we may get? Some program languages have the ability to define a default block that can be used for any type of error. This is known as the 'finally' block and is used to deal with errors that cannot be caught in any of the 'catch' blocks. The 'finally' block is placed after the 'try' and 'catch' blocks. An example of this in C# is given below.

```
string path = @"C:\test.txt";
System.IO.StreamReader file = new
System.IO.StreamReader(path);
char[] buffer = new char[10];
try
    {
file.ReadBlock(buffer, index, buffer.Length);
    }
catch (System.IO.IOException e)
    {
Console.WriteLine("Error reading from file");
    }
finally
    {
      if (file != null)
      {
         file.Close();
      }
    }
```

So in this program we are trying to read from a file called 'test.txt', as per our 'try' block. Unfortunately there are numerous types of errors that can occur when working with files. Because we believe that an I/O error would be the most likely to occur, we defined an 'IOException' in our 'catch' block. But if the 'catch' block never gets called, the error will still slip through and potentially crash the program. For this reason we define a 'finally' block, which will forcefully close the file.

Here's the bottom line when it comes to working with errors.

- Always expect that errors can occur in a program.

- Ensure that you write code to handle all types of error conditions.

30. Logging in Programs

One of the most important concept in programming, is logging of what is happening in the program. Logging helps one to understand how the program is behaving and whether it's performing as per its requirements. In the previous section, we looked at error handling in programs. In order to ensure that these errors are recorded somewhere, we need to have a facility to log the errors. Programming languages provide a few different methods that enable us to log data. We'll look at some of them next.

30.1 Debugging During Development

Some programming languages, such as C#, provide classes that can be used to write debug statements to the console of the Integrated Development Environment as the program runs. This helps give the developer a good insight as to how the program is running. Values, and how they flow in the program, can be seen via these debug statements. For example, the following snippet of code shows how to write a debug statement that outputs to the output window in Visual Studio.

```
class Program
  {
    static void Main(string[] args)
    {
      int i = 5;
      Debug.WriteLine("The value of i is " + i);
      Console.Read();
    }

  }
```

In the above program we are using the 'Debug' class, as well as the 'WriteLine' method in order to write debug statements to the output window. This enables us to see how the code is running. If you have a look at the output window in Visual Studio shown below, you will be able to see the statement written as part of the debug statement.

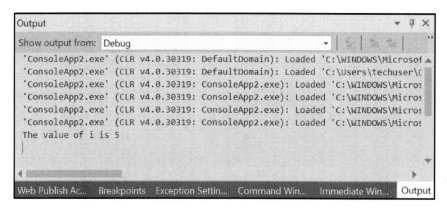

30.2 Tracing after Deployment

Similar to debug statements, trace statements can also be used to write logs during the program's execution. Normally debug statements are used during the development process.

They are used by developers to ensure that the program will run as expected. But trace statements can be used after deploying the program. They are most notably used by administrators to log program behavior in order to ensure that the program continues to run as intended. Trace statements also have the option to generate logging automatically.

30.3 Logging Different Levels

Java has a neat feature that enables you to log different types of events based on different log levels. The log levels define the severity of a message. The 'Level' class is used to define which messages should be written to the log, and contain the following levels in descending order of severity:

- SEVERE (highest)

- WARNING

- INFO

- CONFIG

- FINE

- FINER

- FINEST (lowest)

So if we wanted the program to only log the most severe errors, we would set the logging to 'SEVERE'. This is done by means of the following piece of code:

```
import java.util.logging.Level;
import java.util.logging.Logger;
public class Demo {
    private static final Logger LOGGER =
```

```
Logger.getLogger( Demo.class.getName() );

public static void main(String args[]) {
    LOGGER.log(Level.INFO, "Hello logging");
}}
```

Again, there's no need to dive too deep into this program. Just note the following key points. First, we need to ensure that we import the 'java.util.logging' package. This has the necessary classes used for logging. Then at the top of the class we need to define a 'static' identifier for the logger. Lastly, we set the logging level in the main method before we can start logging.

In conclusion, here are some best practices to follow when logging:

- Try to use one of the existing frameworks for logging, as they already provide a lot of built-in functionality.

- Use a standard structure when you log data. Because at some point in time you would want to analyze the logs, and if they are inconsistent it is going to make your job unnecessarily difficult.

- Ensure to log only what is necessary. If you try to log each and every event, the logs would become large and cumbersome to analyze.

- Ensure that logging happens as a backend process and doesn't slow down your main application.

31. Logical Grouping of Programs

When developing programs that have a long list of requirements, it's possible for the programs to become large and complex, to a point where the code turns into an unmanageable mess. In an earlier chapter we looked at grouping code into various modules. However, sometimes it could also make sense to group programs into separate logical domains.

Programming languages have the capability to group programs into completely separate sections. To illustrate, let's take a simple example of a class called 'Person'. If we needed to have this class separated from other classes in a program, we could use something known as 'namespaces'. A simple code snippet of this concept in C# is shown below.

```
namespace NameA{
    public class Person{
    int ID;
    string Name;
    public void Display(){
    }
    }
}
```

In this program we have a class defined as 'Person', which has attributes and methods. But notice that we now encapsulate the class inside a namespace called 'NameA'. If we wanted to call a function in this class, it would be done in the following way:

```
NameA.Person Per= new NameA.Person();
    clsA.Display();
```

Java also has a similar function known as 'packages' to encapsulate classes. An example of a 'package' is shown below, where we have everything encapsulated inside a package called 'demo'.

```
package demo;
public class Person{
int ID;
string Name;
 public Display(){
   }
}
```

Encapsulating classes provide the following advantages:

- It can be used to categorize classes and interfaces so that they can be easily maintained.

- It can be used to provide access protection.

- In Java, it can eliminate naming collisions. So if we have classes that have the same name, they can be separated into packages so both can exist in the same program.

31.1 Built-in Namespaces

Most programming languages have built-in namespaces with classes inside them. This encapsulation can be used as part of the normal program structure. An example of a simple program in C# is given below.

```
using System;
namespace Demo
{
  class Program
  {
    static void Main(string[] args)
    {
      Console.Read();
    }
  }
}
```

In this program we defined our own namespace 'Demo', however we are also using the built-in 'System' namespace. In order to use the 'System' namespace, we need to use the 'using' keyword in C#. If we didn't use this namespace, the program would simply look as follows:

```
namespace Demo
{
  class Program
  {
    static void Main(string[] args)
    {
      System.Console.Read();
    }
  }
}
```

Now when using the 'Console.Read' statement, we need to prepend the 'System' keyword since the 'Console' class belongs to the 'System' namespace. Here we can see that if we had multiple statements that used the 'System' namespace, it would be inefficient to keep writing the 'System' keyword in front of every statement. That is why we use the 'using' statement to import the System namespace. In Java, we can use the 'import' statement to import classes from certain namespaces. An example is shown below.

```
import java.util.*;
public class ArrayListExample {
  public static void main(String args[]) {
  ArrayList<String> obj = new ArrayList<String>();
  obj.add("Example1");
  obj.add("Example2");
  obj.add("Example3");
}
}
```

In the above example, we need to use a class known as 'ArrayList'. This class is in a namespace called 'java.util'. So in order to use the array list class, we need to use the 'import' statement in order to start using the 'ArrayList' class. As a final note, always ensure that during the design stage of your program, you split your program into multiple units where possible.

32. Deploying Programs

Depending on the type of program that's being developed, the deployment techniques will differ. However the concept of deployment is very important, especially since the world of development is moving more and more towards automation. These days, customers want more features that need to be deployed at a faster rate. When deploying programs the following needs to be kept in mind.

- What is the customer base, and will the application have the capability to be deployed and withstand the high load of customers?

- What is the underlying infrastructure to which the program is being deployed to? Does it have all the necessary components to ensure that the program will work as expected?

- When deploying changes to an existing program, is there any downtime that will be incurred? Are the customers happy with this downtime in the application?

- What is the deployment method that is best suited for the type of application?

32.1 Deployment Mechanisms

If we have a client-server program where the client program needs to be distributed to every workstation, then we need to have a deployment plan in place which can ensure that the client program is distributed as required. This is a big concern when it comes to client-server applications, because you need to ensure that all clients get the same version of the program at the same time.

With web-based applications, we normally need a web server to host the application. Many programming languages use a specific service in order to host the application. For example, C# programs require the Internet Information Services web server. There are different ways to deploy a web program onto a server. When using Visual Studio, you have the option to publish or deploy the web application from the Integrated Development Environment itself. The screenshot below shows the different publishing options that are available for C# in Visual Studio.

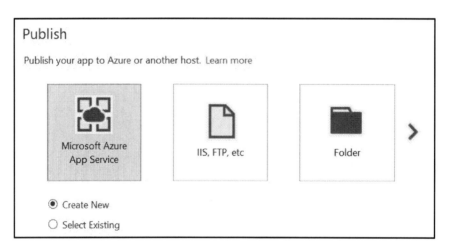

Here we also have the convenient option to deploy applications to the Azure cloud service. Since most applications are now being hosted on the internet, it makes sense to have this option in place. You also have options to deploy the web application directly to the Internet Information Services or to FTP the files on the server for later deployment.

If we now look at Java, there are a couple of methods available for deploying a Java based application. One method involves something known as a 'WAR' package, which bundles the contents of the application together. The 'WAR' file can be created from the IDE or from the command line. This file is then copied onto the web directory, and when the server is restarted it will be unpacked and installed.

32.2 Deploying Program Changes

Normally the first time deployment of a new program is relatively simple. It's the deployment of new features for the program that can become problematic. This is because normally the older version of the program needs to be brought down first and then replaced with the newer version. During this time, users won't be able to access the application. Luckily there are modern day design and deployment techniques available to make the deployment of new features quick and efficient.

Blue-Green deployments

One such technique is the concept of Blue-Green deployments. Normally your current program, which is being used by all users, is referred to as the Blue environment. Then you deploy a new environment, which has the newer version of your application, side by side to your current version. This Green environment is not yet released to the users. Then when the new version needs to be deployed, all users are directed to the Green environment instead of the Blue environment when they log on. Since this is a simple switch, there's no need for any downtime. When all functionality for the newer version has been confirmed, the older environment can be removed.

Containers

Containers are a way of designing and deploying your application into small containers, and there are specialized software that can be used to host these programs. An example of such a design is shown below.

Purchases-v1	Orders-v1

Here we have two functional aspects of an application, which has been split into two separate programs. One is called 'Orders' and the other is called 'Purchases'. Both are running the first version of their programs and are hosted in a container environment. With containers, you can easily launch a new version of one of the programs, let's say the 'Orders' program.

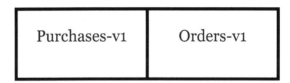

Purchases-v1	Orders-v1	Orders-v2

When the new 'Orders' program has been verified, the older container can be deleted, resulting in the following application.

Purchases-v1	Orders-v2

33. Programming for the Internet

P rogramming for the internet is one of the most challenging aspects for any developer. Your first task is to ensure that the programming language you intend to use has the necessary capabilities to work with the resources on the internet. Fortunately most of the major languages, such as C#, Java, JavaScript, and Angular JS, already have these capabilities built in.

One of the most popular languages being used for web applications nowadays is Angular JS. This is a JavaScript framework that was developed by Google, which has a lot of neat features for web-based applications. Some of those features include:

- Data Binding – This is the action of binding the data layer to the controls on the web page. Without this ability, a lot of code is needed to ensure that the front-end webpage can interact with the associated back-end data. Hence this saves a significant amount of time when developing web applications.

- MVC Behavior – The Model-View-Controller design pattern is adopted by some programming frameworks, and Angular JS is one of them. This allows you to design your 'Model' of data, as well as how the data will be 'Viewed' by the user. Then the 'Controller' is used to decide how the logic will be handled from within the application.

- Directives – Directives can be used to create custom HTML tags that serve as new, custom widgets. They can also be used to 'decorate' elements with behavior and manipulate DOM attributes in interesting ways.

An example of a simple Angular JS program is given below.

```
<!DOCTYPE html>
<html>
<script
src="https://ajax.googleapis.com/ajax/libs/angularjs/1.6.4/angular
.min.js"></script>
<body>
<div ng-app="">
 <p>Please put the name of the Tutorial</p>
<p>Name : <input type="text" ng-model="name"
placeholder="Enter Here"></p>
<h1>The name of the tutorial is {{name}}</h1>
</div>
</body>
</html>
```

When you run this code in a browser, you will initially get the following page:

Please put the name of the Tutorial

Name : [Enter Here]

The name of the tutorial is

Then when you type in the text box, the browser window will automatically pick it up as shown below.

Please put the name of the Tutorial

Name : Angular JS

The name of the tutorial is Angular JS

33.1 Cloud Based Platforms

Another aspect of programming for the internet is cloud-based programming. This is being adopted by a large number of organizations. Cloud-based computing is where services are moved to a third party cloud service rather than having to own and manage them yourself. These services are then completely managed by external vendors. Some of the big players in this space are Amazon Web Services, Google Cloud Services and the Microsoft Azure Platform.

Below are examples of cloud computing components available in one of the most popular platforms, Amazon Web Services.

- Elastic Cloud Computing – This service allows you to manage computing resources on the cloud, such as to provision servers. The underlying physical infrastructure is managed by AWS and you only manage the virtual servers.

- Elastic Block Storage – These are data volumes that can be attached to the virtual servers.

- Simple Storage Services – This is object storage that can be used to store objects such as files, videos and images.

- Elastic Load Balancing – This service can be used to load balance requests to applications.

The best advantage of using these platforms is their high availability and durability. Since the infrastructure is completely managed by the vendor, it removes a lot of headaches for the developer or customer not having to manage the infrastructure.

33.2 IoT

IoT is another concept that is also known as the Internet of Things. This is where everything is connected, such as normal household appliances being connected to the internet. It's basically the need to connect all devices to the internet. Here you would have different sensors installed on devices that would send data across to central hub devices. You would then have the necessary programming languages interpret the data accordingly. Some of the most common programming languages used for IoT programming are:

- C – This is still the most powerful language available for systems based programming. The ability of the libraries available within the C language to interact directly with the hardware is what makes it best suited for working with IoT enabled devices.

- Java – This has always been the most portable language. Hence it can be used on all sorts of chipsets, which are used to build the sensors for IoT based devices. The embedded edition of Java also makes it well suited for IoT based applications.

- Python – This is a simple and powerful programming language. It is pretty light in its implementation and hence is an ideal choice when working with small devices.

The internet domain is continually evolving and the need for digitization is the trend for many organizations. Again, depending on the requirements and the type of application being developed, the right programming language should be chosen. Always take care to ensure that the libraries used in the programming language are not out of date, otherwise this would be a security concern for the application.

34. Serverless Programming

We briefly discussed cloud-based programming in the previous chapter. This type of programming can also be referred to as serverless programming, because we are not managing any infrastructure when implementing applications. In this chapter we will delve a bit deeper into this concept.

Let's say we are building a web-based application in C#. The traditional way to deploy the application would be to have a server that can host the Internet Information Services. But as discussed in the previous chapter, with serverless programming there's no need to create or manage a server. This is all done by an external vendor, such as Amazon Web Services.

But how does this work?

If we take Amazon Web Services as an example, they provide a serverless programming service known as AWS Lambda. When using this service, all you need to do is write the code and upload it. You can then run the code as it is.

Behind the scenes, when you submit a job the service will create a container for executing the code. This container will activate the necessary web server which will be used to execute the code. Once the code has finished execution, the container will be disposed of.

Below is a snapshot that shows an online editor available for AWS Lambda. This editor is used to create a program in the Node.js programming language.

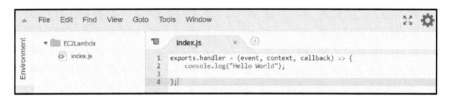

This specific code is a simple string being sent to the console of the program. The editor provides the opportunity to execute the code and also see the output from the program. And all of this is done in the background without the need for provisioning any underlying infrastructure. The Microsoft Azure Platform provides a similar service. So by defining the code below in C#, we can get the resultant output from running it in the cloud as shown on the next page.

```
using System;

public static void Run(TimerInfo myTimer, TraceWriter log)
{
    log.Info("Hello World");
}
```

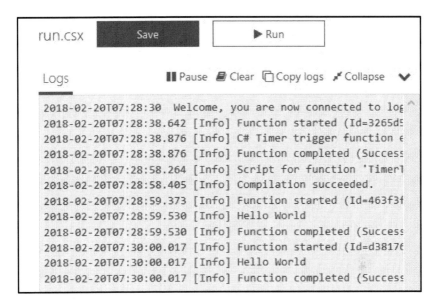

The advantages of using a serverless architecture in the programming world are:

- There's no need to provision the underlying servers required to host web applications. This means that you don't need to pay the initial cost to acquire and set up these servers.

- Since you don't need to manage the underlying infrastructure, you also don't need to maintain the servers. So if a security patch needs to be deployed for the servers, it will be done by the service provider.

- Normally if your application starts getting a lot of requests, you would need to add more server capacity to keep up with the load. But with serverless architecture the provisioning of extra capacity is almost effortless, as the capacity is most likely already available from the service provider.

35. Programming for Mobile Devices

With the popularity and widespread availability of the internet on mobile devices, it has become necessary to ensure that most web-based applications are also compatible with mobile devices. Designing web applications to be mobile friendly is luckily not that hard.

On the Graphical User Interface side of things, there are JavaScript frameworks available which help in designing programs that are mobile friendly. One such example is the Bootstrap framework. This is an open source and free library for designing websites and web-based applications. Bootstrap supports a concept known as responsive web design. This is where web pages are able to render on a variety of devices with varying window and screen sizes.

The program thus needs to automatically detect the underlying device that is used to display and render the webpage accordingly, as well as the window size used. If you take a simple webpage, such as the Amazon webpage for this book, and shrink the dimensions of the page, you will notice that the contents will be shifted in a manner that keeps it displayed properly to the user.

The programming framework should hence also have the ability for this functionality, and this is exactly what the

Bootstrap framework does. In order to apply this functionality to a webpage, you simply need to ensure that the appropriate client libraries are added to the webpage. A simple example is given below.

```
<!DOCTYPE html>
<html lang="en">
<head>
 <title>Bootstrap Example</title>
 <meta charset="utf-8">
 <meta name="viewport" content="width=device-width, initial-scale=1">
 <link rel="stylesheet" href="https://maxcdn.bootstrapcdn.com/bootstrap/3.3.7/css/bootstrap.min.css">
 <script src="https://ajax.googleapis.com/ajax/libs/jquery/3.3.1/jquery.min.js"></script>
 <script src="https://maxcdn.bootstrapcdn.com/bootstrap/3.3.7/js/bootstrap.min.js"></script>
</head>
<body>
<div class="container">
 <h1>This is an example</h1>
</div>
</body>
</html>
```

In the beginning of the code, you will notice references to a few libraries. It is these libraries that ensure that the webpage is able to render under different dimensions. If we were to render the above webpage, it will initially display as follows:

186

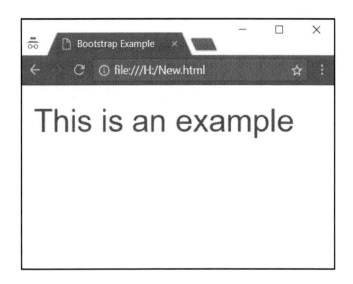

Then if you further reduce the size of the page, it will render as below. Here you will notice that the text on the page has been adjusted to fit the size of the window.

When it comes to mobile app development, you need to choose a programming language based on the mobile operating system you are developing an application for. Let's look at the two most popular operating systems.

35.1 Android

If you want to develop a program that will work on an Android device, then Java is a popular programming language that can be used. The programs for these devices can get pretty complex and one really needs to be an advanced Java programmer to be able to develop these applications. For interest, here is a simple snippet of a Java program for Android. This code is used to add list items to a menu which is displayed on the mobile device.

```java
import android.os.Bundle;
import android.app.Activity;
import android.view.Menu;
import android.widget.ArrayAdapter;
import android.widget.ListView;
public class SimpleListViewActivity extends Activity {
    @Override
    protected void onCreate(Bundle savedInstanceState) {
        super.onCreate(savedInstanceState);
        setContentView(R.layout.activity_simple_list_view);
        String[] myStringArray = { "Option1", " Option2", "
Option3" };
        ArrayAdapter<String> adapter = new
ArrayAdapter<String>(this,
        R.layout.simple_list_view_item, myStringArray);

        ListView listView = (ListView) findViewById(R.id.lvDemo);
        listView.setAdapter(adapter);
    }
    @Override
    public boolean onCreateOptionsMenu(Menu menu) {
    getMenuInflater().inflate(R.menu.activity_simple_list_view,
menu);
        return true;
    }
}
```

35.2 iOS

This is the underlying operating system for all Apple devices. If you want to develop mobile applications for this operating system, then a popular programming language would be Swift. Again, you need to be well versed in Swift to develop mobile applications. But don't let this put you off mobile app development. All you need is enough practice in the appropriate language.

We don't cover Swift programming at the moment, but we do have a complete series on Java Programming to help you get started.

36. Design Practices

In this final chapter we will have a look at the design stage of the development process and some best practices to keep in mind. When creating applications, we normally go through a development lifecycle. The different stages of a typical development lifecycle for an application are shown below.

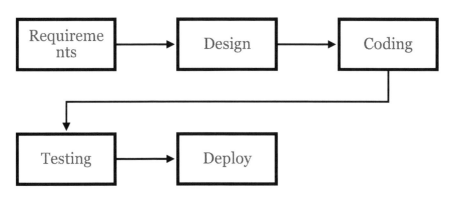

First, we need to gather the requirements for our application to understand what the application is meant to do. This can come from the client, the project manager, end users or developers. Once the requirement gathering phase is completed, we move onto the design stage where we need to ensure that the application is designed according to the requirements. This is one of the most important stages of the lifecycle, since it lays the foundation for our coding.

After this phase, we have the coding, testing and deployment of the application. Due to the importance of the design stage, there are a few core design principles to take note of, which we will look at next.

Split the application into multiple layers

Try to introduce multiple layers in the design of your application. This can lead to better and easier maintenance by isolating code into various layers and segments. Each section can also be tested separately, which makes the development process so much easier.

Manage components as individual services

This is always a good design practice. By having each component as a service, it becomes easier to share the same service across multiple applications and hence makes for better reusability. So for example, if your application has three modules such as Customers, Orders and Purchases, you can design them as independent services.

Customers Service	Orders Service	Purchases Service

Decouple the application components

It is important to ensure that application components in your architecture are not tightly coupled. This is also in line with the previous design practice. If you have dependencies between multiple components of your application, then changes to your application can become difficult.

If you make changes to one component, you might have unforeseen issues in another dependent component of your application.

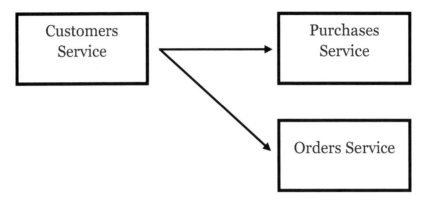

Ensure the application can be tested at a later point in time

It is possible for applications to become so complex that testing becomes problematic. Luckily some programming languages are built with testing in mind, such as Angular JS. The Angular JS framework has testing frameworks such as Karma and Jasmine to complement the development framework. Below is an example of a unit testing code created in the Jasmine framework. This code is just used to ensure that a set of options that is presented to the user is set as OptionA, OptionB and OptionC.

```
describe('Sample Test', function() {
 it('Testing options', function() {
  var users = ['OptionA', 'OptionB', 'OptionC'];
  var sorted = sortOptions(options);
  expect(sorted).toEqual(['OptionA', 'OptionB', 'OptionC']);
 });
});
```

Make sure the application is portable

If you plan to deploy your application in multiple environments, then your application should be able to adapt to the various operating systems and devices. Java is a popular language that is portable in nature and can work on multiple operating system platforms.

Ensure there is support for the programming language

This becomes important when deciding which programming language is most suitable at the design stage. So in addition to looking at which language fits all requirements, it's also important to ensure that it has enough support from multiple communities. This ensures that there are regular updates to bug fixes, but also support for if you get stuck in any way.

Conclusion

This brings us to the end of this guide. I hope that you enjoyed learning more about the world of programming, and how powerful and versatile it can be. Programming has become one of the most valuable skills you can learn today. Not only in your professional life, but in your personal life as well. I can't count how many times I've written a small script to help me with my daily tasks. It is something you can use for the rest of your life.

"What's next" you might ask? By now you probably have an idea of which programming language you have a preference for. If not, have a re-look at Chapter 4 which summarizes the main aspects of the most popular languages. You really can't go wrong with any of these languages. But if you are still undecided, I suggest just trying one out. If you don't like it, you can simply move on to the next one.

The most important part of learning any programming language, is practice. Practical examples are proven to be the best way to learn a programming language, which is why I try to cram as many examples as possible into my guides. If you want to learn any of the popular languages in a step-by-step way that is tailored specifically for beginners, be sure to check out any of the series below.

Good luck and happy programming!

PYTHON

Programming Basics for Absolute Beginners

a, FREE Kindle Version with Paperback

C++

Programming Basics for Absolute Beginners

a, FREE Kindle Version with Paperback

JAVA

Programming Basics for Absolute Beginners

a, FREE Kindle Version with Paperback

C#
Programming Basics for Absolute Beginners

JAVASCRIPT
Programming Basics for Absolute Beginners

SQL
Programming Basics for Absolute Beginners

About the Author

Nathan Clark is an expert programmer with nearly 20 years of experience in the software industry.

With a master's degree from MIT, he has worked for some of the leading software companies in the United States and built up extensive knowledge of software design and development.

Nathan and his wife, Sarah, started their own development firm in 2009 to be able to take on more challenging and creative projects. Today they assist high-caliber clients from all over the world.

Nathan enjoys sharing his programming knowledge through his book series, developing innovative software solutions for their clients and watching classic sci-fi movies in his free time.

Printed in Great Britain
by Amazon